CALLING
the SH⊕TS

CALLING
the SHOTS

SELF-PROTECTION AND FIREARM CHOICES THAT WORK FOR YOU

JENNA MEEK

CARRY ON PUBLISHING

Carry On Publishing
4833 Front Street, Unit B-267
Castle Rock, CO 80104

Cover and interior design, Kamila Miller
Cover Art- Doug Wittrock, Bokeh Images
Photos by Doug Wittrock (unless otherwise noted)
Editor: Jocelyne Thomas, Branwen Books Editing

First Edition
ISBN-13: 978-0692626580
ISBN-10: 0692626581

Disclaimer: The contents of this book contain the personal story and experiences of the author. The information presented in the book should not be misconstrued as legal advice. Please take great care in your self-protection and firearms education and if you should decide to employ strategies that the author has laid out in these pages, use common sense and above all else, keep it safe!

Contents

ACKNOWLEDGEMENTS

I am fortunate to have become part of a network of amazing people on my self-defense and teaching journey and lots of them have selflessly provided me with their time, talents and advice. Not to mention a lot of encouragement!

Many thanks to the following people who provided help to me throughout this lengthy process:

Gila Hayes, Firearms Academy of Seattle

Julie Hoffman

Kathy Jackson, Cornered Cat LLC.

Marc MacYoung, No Nonsense Self-Defense

Kamila Miller

Rory Miller, Chiron Training/Conflict Communications

Ashley Nicol

Doug Wittrock, *Bokeh Images*

And most of all, thanks to my husband, Jeff Meek. My biggest supporter (who is always there with a kind word or a swift kick in the pants depending on what type of encouragement I need on any given day). Without Jeff's gentle persuasion to get into the firearms training profession and encouragement to become an author this book would never have happened!

FOREWORD

If you believe the world is always safe, you have been lied to. But it's just as big of a lie to believe the world is always dangerous. It's not. Having said that, the world *can be* an unsafe place. Overwhelmingly it's not, but there are times. Knowing this gives you more options. More ways of handling both.

You can do a lot to reduce both dangers to yourself and your chances of being involved with violence with good lifestyle choices. For example don't associate with violent people and/or people involved in illegal activities. Yes, it's really that simple. Another good rule of thumb for preventing physical violence is don't be verbally or emotionally violent to others. This last is actually harder than the first. Many people use words as weapons. They rely on insults, hostile words, anger and attitude to scare off potential trouble. That's a strategy that works until it doesn't. In which case they discover —the hard way— that violent words and emotions do not trump physical violence. In fact, they kind of provoke it.

But there's an interesting side note to that. That is how often people who rely on harsh words, outrage and attitude to keep them safe, rebel at the very idea of being polite. They interpret the advice "be polite" as disarming them. Then always comes the inevitable, "but what if being polite doesn't work? "Or my favorite rationalization for being hostile and selfish, "If I'm polite people will think I'm weak." Funny, but speaking from the receiving end, that's not how it comes across — especially if I'm willing to use physical violence as a response to your verbal violence.

Oddly enough, when you choose a firearm for personal protection, you'll find good manners and being nice are your first lines of defense in not having to shoot someone. And if they don't work — especially when you've mixed them with setting boundaries — it's an indicator that something is not right with the situation. As in there's something else going on there — something not good.

In the movie "Open Range" ex-gunslinger Charley Waite makes an observation, "Most times a man will tell you his bad intentions if you let yourself listen." Someone breaking social rules and scripts is often them telling you their bad intentions. The difference is unlike relying on good manners, social expectation and — in a pinch — harsh words to keep you safe, choosing self-protection gives you another option when those don't work.

Sad truth is, although rare, there are times you're going to need another option. You can be the best, nicest, and most caring person in the world, still sometimes bad things happen. When — and God forbid it should happen — they do, it helps to have more options than just to call for help. There's an old saw in the self-defense world "When seconds count, the police are only minutes away." That is another sad, but true fact of life. Choosing the option self-protection goes a long way to making sure you're still healthy when the police finally arrive.

Jenna Meek came onto my radar a few years ago and I saw in her many of the things I'm not. First a woman. Second a mother. Third, a nice person. Those three things make her much, much more accessible to women who want to learn about personal safety. Also someone who understands the concerns, hesitations and socialization that women face regarding personal safety. Issues that — speaking as an ex-streetfighter and violence professional — hadn't been issues for me for decades, if at all. I have no qualms about defending myself or others. That it could even be a question gets a confused Neanderthal look and a questioning "URH? " sound from me. But you're not me. She can help guide you through the hesitations and moral quandaries. She also can address subjects knowledgeably that I'd never considered. For example, how does wearing a dress or your bust size affect where and how you carry? Seriously, that's never been an issue for me.

Another issue for many women when it comes to learning about firearms is …well, 'The Macho.'

Simply stated, if you have the strength to open a can of soup, you're strong enough to defend yourself against the largest man. So big and strong is not the issue, mindset is. As Jenna points out, she's not here to teach you how to be tacti-kool. Nor does she expect you to dedicate your life into obsessing on the details and intricacies of shooting as so many men do. It's just not that big of a part of your life. Nor should it be. Having said that, in the piles and piles of minutia and testosterone, there as some key points you need to know. Once you know these general points, the whole process of learning and making the best choices for you become much, much easier.

The idea of taking responsibility for your personal safety can be both scary and daunting. That, more than it could become necessary, is the bad news. The good news is you hold in your hands a book written by someone who understands and can help you get through the rough spots.

Marc MacYoung

If you know who I am,
that's enough. If you
don't, it would take too
long to explain. Besides,
you have better ways to
spend your time.

INTRODUCTION

So you want to get a gun and learn how to use it safely and responsibly. Great! You've come to the right place! I have struggled with *all* of the concepts that we will discuss in this book. I believe it's my calling to help others who are facing the same questions and issues I grappled with on my journey to owning firearms. It had never crossed my mind to own or carry guns, or become a firearms instructor. Once I did, it took me a while to realize that I was in a unique position to help people –especially women- just like me. I think it's important to have someone that you can relate to when it comes to guns. I am a mom who carries a gun and loves knowing that I possess the skills and tools I need to protect myself and my family.

Let me tell you a little bit about myself and why I believe I can help you on *your* journey. Bear with me; I am not a big fan of talking about myself. Here goes…!

My firearms journey started in 2007. This was just after my only child was born. My husband, Jeff, decided that he wanted to get back into shooting after taking some time off from the sport. I was a little leery of this idea. I was not afraid of guns and I had shot guns a couple of times in my life, but I just didn't see the need to have guns in the house. This is a funny concept to me now.

The next thing I knew, Jeff got a gun. When this happened, I decided that I should probably know how to use it, if it was going to be in the house. So Jeff gave me a crash course in how it worked. We also found an article on the internet titled, "How to Rack the Slide." This article taught me the proper technique to rack any slide (pulling back the slide to chamber a round) with ease. As time went on, I read every article on that amazing website, which is still around today. You may have heard of it; CorneredCat[1], the creation of the talented and capable Kathy Jackson, who also runs her own firearms training company by the same name.

After the crash course and learning how to rack a slide, we were off to the indoor shooting range. I picked up Jeff's gun and fired about five rounds. I couldn't tell you if I even hit the target or not, but I can tell you that I set the gun down on the bench and walked off the range – shaking.

I told Jeff that I never wanted to shoot that big old gun again. He looked at me with despair in his eyes and wanted to know what had gone wrong. I told him that his gun was "miserable." It was too big to comfortably fit in my hands; it was loud and had a lot of recoil. I was done with it!

That, my friends, is where I think many women give up. I think the reason for this is simply because this sort of thing can be intimidating. If learning firearms was not your idea to begin with it, makes it that much harder to stay involved when the experience is not pleasant. Maybe you had someone encouraging you to learn about guns and/or shooting, and instead of the wonderful experience you were told about, you had a disappointing or frustrating experience similar to mine. There is a ton to learn, and until we have had some exposure to the sport of shooting we may not be ready to trust the information that we are given. We may want to investigate these claims for ourselves. This takes practice and in many cases, trial and error. The idea of using a gun, whether for sport or something more serious such as self-defense, is a big decision. This is not something we can decide to do one day and have all the knowledge and skills we need to make it happen the next. It is a process. But if you can stay with it, the end results can be very rewarding and empowering. Since you are reading a book I've written about this process, you already know that walking off the range that day is not where my story ends. This is one time that being stubborn was a blessing in

---

1   http://www.corneredcat.com/

disguise. I am certain that there are more examples of this in my life, but this is the one that stands out most to me.

About a week after this incident, I decided that if we were going to have a gun in the house, I needed to know how to use it, and I had to do so on my own terms. That is when I went out and bought my own gun. Jeff came along for the ride, but he let me do the shopping.

I remember this day just like it was yesterday. We went to a local gun store and there were some older gentlemen working behind the counter that day. Little did I know that working with the old guys would actually become enjoyable. On this day, however, it was completely intimidating. Here I was trying to buy a gun when I didn't even know what I didn't know! I was sure that the guys working the counter would "… have just what you need, little lady." It's like taking the car in for an oil change and fighting to decline all the extra services that "you have to have."

I told the guys that I was in the market for a gun and that I wanted something small and easy to manage. (Ha! This is counterproductive; I just didn't know it at the time.) I told them that I wanted something I could learn to use and could shoot with every now and then. I told them I was not planning on using it regularly but since we were going to have Jeff's gun in the house, I wanted to be familiar with how they work and have one that suited me. They tried to sell me a Baby Eagle. This was the first time, but not the last that this gun store tried to persuade me to buy a Baby Eagle. For the next year and a half, each time I walked through their door or called to inquire about something being in stock they tried to sell me a Baby Eagle. Finally I just stopped going there.

At this stage in the game, I had no idea how to shop for a gun. In the course of your reading, I'll provide the information you need in order to be a savvier gun shopper than I was that first time.

Buying my own gun was just what I needed to get my interest going. I ended up purchasing a Fabrique Nationale Herstal (FNP) FNP-9. The gun is chambered in 9mm, which

I found a whole lot easier for a newbie to shoot than the .40 Smith & Wesson (S&W) Jeff used. At the time, I thought this was going to be a great gun for me. It seemed to fit my hand well enough and that was a start. The best part about the FN was that the recoil was manageable for me. The noise didn't seem a scary to me either, although I am sure that was all in my head.

A few weeks later I found myself in my first firearms class. This is the same week that I bought my second gun, a Springfield Armory Enhanced Micro Pistol (EMP) that I named Lucy. For those of you keeping score at home, I now owned more guns than my husband. That might be why my first instructor nicknamed me 'Annie Oakley'!

The interesting thing about purchasing that second gun is that in just a short period of time I started to learn how this stuff – guns and the mechanics of the gun – works. I also realized as soon as I had some formal training under my belt that the FN might not be such a good match for me, and sometime later I ended up selling it. Lucy and I are still BFF's though!

CALLING
the SHOTS

WHY I TEACH

A big part of the reason I teach about firearms is because when I took over the day-to-day operations of Carry On Colorado, I got a ton of phone calls from women, and a lot of them went something like this:

Caller: "Hi, I see on your website that you'll take me gun shopping."

Me: "Yes, that's right; as a free service to our students we'd love to help you through the process of buying a gun."

Caller: "Okay, great! I want to take your next class, but can you take me to the gun store right now? "

Me: "Well, before we do that let me ask you a couple of questions.... Do you have any experience with handguns? "

Caller: "Um, No. That's why I want to take a class with you."

Me: "That is a great first step. Next question: What will you use the gun for? "

Caller: "Oh, that's easy, I want it for home defense. I am going to keep it in my night stand."

Me: "Okay, also great. [Assuming that this is not a place that unauthorized persons can get to the gun; in my house that doesn't work, as I have a little one]. Since you said you want to take a Carrying a Concealed Weapon (CCW) class with me, do you ever intend to carry this gun on your person? "

Caller: "Of course I am planning to carry this gun on my person!"

Me: "Ah ha! This is why I need you to take the class *before* we can go buy you a gun. You don't in fact want a 'home defense' or 'night stand' gun at all. What you really want is a 'carry' gun that you will keep by your bed. So this gun will be able to serve many purposes."

As this conversation shows, you have to have a clear idea of what the main purpose of your firearm will be. However, until you have someone you can trust and who's been there to teach you what you don't even know you *need* to know, how will you decide on that purpose? That, my friends, is "*why* I do this!"

As an aside, I'll mention that there is no right or wrong answer with regards to purpose. In my opinion, though, a carry gun and a home defense gun can be two different animals. For me, a carry gun has to small and lightweight enough that I will actually carry it with me when I leave the house. Case in point: I fell in love with 1911s early on in my firearms journey.

> **TIP:** If you are new to guns, I applaud you for having the courage to learn something new! Before you rush out and buy a gun just to get into the game, however, you need to first learn what you **don't** know. What I mean by this is that you need to take a class from a reputable instructor, talk to people who know guns and learn what questions you should be asking about before you make that purchase.

I love them! Best gun on the planet, if you ask me. So I went out and bought a Springfield Armory EMP chambered in 9mm as my carry gun. It just might be the best gun that Jeff and I own collectively, which says a lot. That said, it's way too heavy for me to comfortably carry every day. Needless to say, I was never completely comfortable carrying this gun. So I ended up with a Kahr PM9 for every day carry (EDC). It was small, lightweight and the best part was I would have it with me whenever I left the house. I have recently switched to carrying a Glock 43, as it has all the same characteristics as the Kahr PM9, with the addition of a much nicer trigger. Alternatively, a home defense gun can be anything you want it to be. If I didn't have to worry about children running around I'd probably keep an AR-15 next to the bed.

If you are like me and think that guns are like shoes and one pair just isn't enough, then go for it. Remember though, it's better to make sure those shoes fit before you wear them out of the store than to get blisters because the shoes were so cute that we bought them even though they were ill-fitting. C'mon, we've all been there!

My job as a firearms instructor is not to turn you into a special forces, tactical operator or some Hollywood stunt woman; in fact, it is quite the opposite! I want to help you achieve your goals, whatever those may be. Maybe you just want to leave the house to go shopping and be able to protect yourself if trouble strikes or maybe you just want to hit the bull's eye of a target 15 yards away. No matter what your goals are, I think you will benefit from the experience I have gained in my foray into the world of guns. I applaud your courage for picking up this book. I am here to let you know, dear reader, that guns don't have to be scary and you don't have to act like and train like a Navy SEAL to be safe and effective with guns. There are good places we can go together by applying the topics that we'll discuss in this book to our everyday lives as women who want the means to defend ourselves if we ever need to.

The media– and even parts of the well-meaning "gun culture" can make guns seem like big scary objects that we must fear. We've all heard the media talk about those ", assault rifles" and "high capacity magazines" for example. Some of you may even have a "drunken uncle" who carries a gun and treats it with little or no respect at the family reunion. Maybe he takes it out to show you how harmless it is while it's loaded, and doesn't pay attention to the direction of the muzzle. Whatever the case may be, in doing these things guns and the "gun community" in general are given a bad name. The term "gun nut" is used a lot to describe these people with unsafe gun habits, but it is also used in reference to responsible gun owners. I really don't appreciate that term.

When I was learning about guns my husband was my first real resource. He is a great teacher. He is patient, knowledgeable and genuinely interested in helping people learn about firearms and self-defense. I am lucky to have such a great teacher on my journey! I will also tell you that unless your husband is a firearm professional (and even sometimes if he is) that having your husband teach you to shoot is not always a great idea. For example, I would never let Jeff teach me how to golf. (No offense, Dear, it's just not a good idea; I want to like you at the end of the day!) Learning to shoot or learning to golf can be frustrating and it might be better to learn from an impartial third party. I really have to applaud the men that I come across that are looking to get the ladies in their lives to learn how to shoot but want no part of the teaching. This takes a secure guy. Keep up the good work, fellas!

It didn't take me long, however, to realize that if I was going to jump into gun ownership and the shooting sports with both feet, then just taking what my husband told me and running with it was not going to cut it. You see, there is so much to this hobby (for some of us, it's a lifestyle) that you really need to do this for yourself.

WHY CARRY A GUN?

The following quote by Col. Jeff Cooper pretty much sums it up: "I was once asked by a lady visiting if I had a gun in the house. I said I did. She said 'Well I certainly hope it isn't loaded! 'To which I said, 'Of course it is loaded, it can't work without bullets! 'She then asked, 'Are you that afraid of someone evil coming into your house? ' My reply was, "No not at all. I am not afraid of the house catching fire either, but I have fire extinguishers around, and they are all loaded too."

The point of this quote is that we all do things that prepare us for our daily lives. These things often times are not even given a second thought. Some examples of this are wearing a seatbelt when we get into the car. I don't climb into my car every day thinking, 'well, I'd better buckle up because today is the day I am going to need this seatbelt'. We also have all kinds of insurance to help protect us from financial and legal problems if the time ever comes. I carry home, auto, life and professional insurance policies, just to name a few. I should hope that I'll never have to use them, but they are there to protect me and my family if something ever goes horribly wrong. This also goes for me carrying a gun. I sure hope I never have to use it, but I will have it if I ever need it.

I don't carry a gun because it is comfortable or because I like the challenge of trying to conceal the darn thing. For me, having a gun is comforting because I feel that having a gun levels the playing field. I am not a large person with a lot of strength and having a gun makes me feel like I could take care of myself or my loved ones if it ever came to that. It took me a long time to get to the point where I was comfortable carrying a gun. I had hours of training and practice. I also felt that knowing the laws associated with gun ownership was a 'must'. You have to know the rules of the road, as it were. Once I felt like I had a good understanding of these concepts, I was able to move on to how to actually function in my daily life with a gun on my person. I will go into great detail on these topics in subsequent chapters of this book. I mentioned that I carry a gun to level the playing field between me and potential scum-bags. Another reason I carry a gun is because I have learned that *my* safety is *my* responsibility. Did you know that as ruled in many court cases [2][3]that law enforcement has no legal obligation to protect you? I'll give you a minute to re-read that part. For some of us, this is the exact opposite of what we have always believed to be true. But, think about it for a minute. When a crime occurs when do the police usually show up? That's right; they show up after the crime has been committed. Or if it's a bad day for the bad guys, maybe the police will happen upon a crime already in progress and are able to thwart the crime mid-way through. I for one have never seen a news story about crimes that were stopped before any crime had been committed. It just doesn't happen that way. The reason for this is because most criminals are smart enough not to commit crimes in the presence of a police officer and the police only get called after something bad has happened. Their job is to figure out what happened and find the bad guys and help bring them to justice after-the-fact.

2   Castle Rock, Colorado v. Gonzales (04-278) 545 U.S. 748 (2005). http://tinyurl.com/jag7uu5

3   Warren v. District of Columbia http://tinyurl.com/gwbtbpp

With that said, please don't misunderstand me. I love the police and law enforcement! They are out there every day risking their lives and trying to keep bad guys off the streets. I wouldn't want to do that job for anything. They are also great at what they do. But it's our job to take care of ourselves. Yes, the police have a duty to act. However, what if you are out of jurisdiction when the call is made to the authorities, or if there is a mass casualty event at the same time as that fender-bender you just got into? In those cases the police may have larger things to deal with then helping ONE person. The job of law enforcement is to take care of the community before they can take care of an individual. It's not the job of the police to keep us safe. Please think about this: *your* safety is *your* responsibility. This is why I carry a gun.

Some of you may be reading this with the hopes of coming to some sort of conclusion of what is the right decision for your self-defense plan. I think this book and the experiences that I am about to share with you are an excellent resource for you on this part of your journey. The more information you are able to gather the better prepared you will be to make that decision for yourself. I would be remiss if I did not pose the following question to you. First, some background; in the first firearms class I ever took my instructor was an older gentleman who had been around guns his whole life. He's been around so much lead that he had to add a mask and protective gloves to his safety equipment; he was hard-core and he had a heart of gold. You could tell that he really cared about his students. He left a mark on me, for sure. That's hard to do. One question he posed to us, and I am now posing to you, Dear Reader, is this: "Are you capable of taking a human life? " He told us to think long and hard about this and be able to look ourselves in the mirror and answer that question. He said that if our answer was "no," that that was ok, but that we would have no business carrying a gun. If that is the case you have a responsibility to yourself and to society to find another self-defense tool.

That really struck me. Now that I am years beyond that first class, I get it. A firearm in the hand of someone who is unwilling or unprepared to use it is more dangerous to that person than being unarmed.

So, if you come to the conclusion that a gun is not the tool for you that is just fine. You will be much better served with something else in your tool box. There is no shame in that. But I do encourage you to figure this out before it's too late.

How to Buy a Gun

The question I am asked most frequently is "How do I buy a gun? " My answer to this is that there is no easy answer, unfortunately. Buying a gun is a very personal experience. It's like the difference between buying COACH or a Dooney and Bourke handbag, or red wine vs. white wine. I happen to appreciate a COACH bag and a glass of dry red wine, but that doesn't mean that Dooney's and white wine are bad, they just don't suit my taste as well. The same holds true with guns.

I have already mentioned that I carry a Glock 43. I carry this gun because it is one of the smallest 9mm pistols that I have enjoyed shooting. At first I was worried about concealing the G43 because it was bigger than the gun I had been carrying, but I love the size of this gun. It is perfect for me to easily conceal and it is also something that I am comfortable shooting. These are the selling points.

When you walk into a gun store some, but not all, of the employees will be men. And some, but not all, of those men will see you coming and immediately point you to the small, cute little revolvers or pink guns with that *Hey little lady, I have just the thing for you* gleam in their eye. Most men just assume that you will not be able to rack a slide or manipulate a semi-auto, but they couldn't be more wrong about that! I have to say that years ago this was a lot more common than it is today. If you happen to be in the market for one of these guns (and there is nothing wrong with that; remember, it is about personal preference), you're in luck! If not, then keep reading.

Many times we have this idea of the *perfect* gun. I am sorry to break this to you, but I am not sure that the *perfect* gun actually exists. In my assessment there is usually a trade off or two that we make when purchasing guns (and holsters, for that matter). My advice is to make a list of pros and cons. You don't have to write one out, just make an honest effort to think about what you like and don't like about the gun. When you find a gun with cons that you can live with, you will be on the right track.

There are a lot of factors in selecting a pistol. These can include:

- The intended purpose of the pistol
- Price and budget
- Availability and price of ammunition
- Pistol fit and ergonomics
- Pistol size and weight
- Recoil
- Simplicity of operation and ease of cleaning
- Reputation of manufacturer
- Warranty or Guarantee
- Availability of repair of aftermarket parts

I like to equate the gun buying process to that of buying a car. This analogy seems to work well for men and women alike. When I buy a car I have to have an idea of what I will use the car for (Do I need an SUV or do I want a sports car?) and it has to fit me! When I say it has to *fit me* what I mean is that it has to fit my physical self, as I am only 5' tall: if the driver's seat is so deep that it makes the pedals hard to reach then that's not the car for me! Once I find a car that fits me physically I can start to determine what bells and whistles I need (air conditioning, memory seats) and what I can live without (navigation and overhead DVD) for example.

My first car was an older model Chevy Cavalier. My parents had a friend who was selling it and I ended up with this car sight unseen. (My Dad had seen and checked out the car, but I hadn't.) I was extremely excited to get my first car, right up until the part where I slipped behind the steering wheel for the first time. The good news was that if I pulled the seat all the way up (remember that I am 5-foot-nothing) I could reach the pedals. The bad news was that I couldn't see over the steering wheel! The worst news was that the car had already been bought and delivered. If I remember correctly I cried for a long while over this. I sat on a phone book to drive the damn thing. I think I eventually found some kind of cushion or pillow to replace that phone book, but the damage had already been done. Everyone that knew me well knew that I had to sit on a phone book to see over the steering wheel of my own car – and now so do you. Now you also know why finding a car that fits you is so important; not just for being spared a colossal amount of embarrassment, but for safety reasons as well.

I will mention again that it's the same for guns. Not only am I short, but I also have tiny hands. This is a sticking point when it comes to finding a gun that fits me. If the grips are too big I can't reach the trigger. I have yet to find a gun with grips that are too small, but that could also be an issue, as having too much finger on the trigger can mean that you need to make adjustments to be able to shoot properly.

Figure 1: This small revolver has nice small grips that work well for little hands.

*Figure 2: Sub-compact guns also fit small
hands nicely. This is me with my Kahr.*

*Figure 3: Here I am with Lucy, my
Springfield EMP. This gun fits just right!*

*Figure 4: This photo shows how big a double
stack .45ACP 1911 really is for me.*

Since I have tiny hands I cannot comfortably shoot a double stack Glock, for example. Yes it has a larger capacity, but it's like getting my hand around a peanut butter jar. That's not to say if a double stack Glock were the only thing there when I reached for a gun in desperate times that I *couldn't* shoot it or be accurate with it. It is just not my first choice. I'll mention that this is actually just fine by me. Has anyone ever shot a Glock 19 and *not* had the shell casing come back and hit them square in the forehead or slip down the front of their shirt? With me and this particular gun, I get hit in the forehead every time! I know I am not alone in this experience! There is nothing that screams *danger* like doing the hot brass dance on the firing line!

So let's get to the part about buying a gun, shall we?

TIP: *If you don't know, the hot brass dance is what usually happens if a hot shell casing finds its way into the neckline of your shirt. Lots of people will dance around waving a gun trying to alleviate the burning sensation of the hot brass meeting flesh, thus, causing a dangerous situation on the range. In some cases, I have seen hot brass go down the back of a shirt collar and land in a delicate area inside the pants. This also usually ends in a hot brass dance. This is one of the reasons why shooters are encouraged to wear a hat with a visor and closed collars while shooting.*

The first step to buying a gun, like buying a car is to know what it will be used for. I am talking about the primary purpose here. Yes, guns can serve more than one purpose. Is this a gun that you will carry with you either on your person or in a purse? Maybe the main purpose of the gun will be home protection or for target practice. All of these purposes are great. We just need to narrow it down because it makes all the difference in the world when choosing the type of gun to buy.

When I refer to a 'carry gun' I am talking about something that is small enough and light enough to carry on my person. This same gun can absolutely also be used for 'home defense' or as a 'bump in the night gun' – there is no question about that. Many times when people refer to a gun as a 'home defense weapon' they are referring to a gun that they are not going to carry regularly, if ever. Home defense guns by nature tend to be larger and maybe heavier than their smaller counter parts. Often times the home defense gun will be able to hold more rounds as well. For me, these larger guns are harder to carry, but many people are able to pull it off without an issue. My husband is a big guy and he is able to carry a much larger and heavier gun than what is comfortable for me to carry.

Now that you know what you will use this gun for we can look at what size to get. A "carry" gun will need to be small and light weight enough to carry with you. Yes, even if you are keeping it in your night stand and using it as your home protection gun it's still a "carry" gun first if you ever plan to carry it. If it's too big and heavy you might just be like me and decide to leave it behind. This is why I personally have more than one gun. I do have one that is small, lightweight and goes with me most all of the time. If you have no intention of ever carrying it anywhere but the shooting range for practice than you might just get away with a full size model of gun. There is no right or wrong here; it's all about your personal preference and what you're going to use it for.

Whether to choose a semi-automatic or a revolver is another consideration. There are distinct advantages and disadvantages to each. Let's consider the advantages and disadvantages of the revolver first. The revolver is a no-nonsense gun. There are only a few moving parts and handling malfunctions with a revolver are as easy as can be to deal with unless the malfunction stems from a mechanical issue (something is broken). That is when you will have a real problem, as a gunsmith is the only one who can fix that issue. If you are in a self-defense situation you won't have that kind of time. Revolvers also tend to have smaller grips (a pro or a con, depending on the size of your hands).

The cons are that they have a capacity of 5 or 6 rounds, can be tricky to reload in a hurry and often times have sights that are difficult to see. I have also met many people (women especially) who get little, lightweight revolvers thinking that they are the answer to all of their prayers – *until they shoot them*. The running consensus here is that most often there is a lot of recoil felt and firing more than a box of ammo is a tall order. The reason so many people run into this with the small, lightweight guns (and it's not just revolvers) is that there is less mass on the gun to absorb the recoil. This means all that energy has to go somewhere and we tend to feel it more in our hands and wrists.

In contrast to revolvers, semi-autos can have different size grips available for a given model. Lots of models of semi-automatic pistols come with a set of interchangeable backstraps for different sized hands. While it is less common, some handgun models also come with interchangeable front straps and/or side panels making these grips customizable to the shooter. Some semi-autos may have a higher capacity

TIP: *All too often I hear people telling women that they need to shoot a revolver because it is easier to manipulate. This is not necessarily true. The fact is that revolvers don't have a slide to rack and that may be easier. However, most of the time when women have issues racking a slide it is because of a physical limitation or — more common— lack of technique. The technique can be taught and mastered with some practice. The problem I see with this advice is that if women have physical limitations that would prevent them from racking a slide, it may have something to do with a lack of grip strength. If this is the case pulling the long heavy trigger pull on a revolver is going to also be a tall order.*

depending on the size of the gun, and they can have external safety features (again, this could be considered a pro or con depending on your preferences). Semi-autos also tend to be faster and easier to reload than revolvers (although, this really depends on how much you practice with your weapon. I have seen some revolver shooters who are very fast on the reload).

On the down side, there are more moving parts and more manipulation is needed to shoot a semi-automatic pistol than a revolver, including racking the slide, loading magazines and having to manually clear any malfunctions you might have. Luckily there are some really good techniques out there that will help you do these manipulations as efficiently as possible. With practice you can get really good at all of these things, whether you choose a revolver or a semi-automatic pistol.

TIP: If you are looking to purchase a semi-automatic pistol that comes with interchangeable grip parts there is no harm in asking the sales person to help you check these out and try them on for size in the store **before** making your purchase. My philosophy is that it's better to be safe than sorry. You don't want to end up with a gun that doesn't fit (or a car in which you can't see over the steering wheel, for that matter).

Now that we have determined what size (and maybe style) of gun we want, we can start the process of touch and feel. This is the fun part. Head out to the gun store and actually handle whatever they have in stock in your range of sizes. Yes, guns come in many sizes ranging from sub-compact to full-size for semi autos, and small or J-frame to full size for revolvers. Don't worry about cartridge designation at this point.

Wait a minute, did you catch that? I said "cartridge designation". Yes, the use of that term was intentional. I promise to get into more detail on this in another chapter because ammunition is its own beast. But for now, let's keep handling some guns in the correct size range and find something that fits our hand. The fit is the key. If a gun is too big (double stack .45) or too small (revolver with a tiny grip) then we might never be truly comfortable shooting it.

Figure 5: A size comparison of the Springfield XD series of pistols. Pictured top to bottom is a full size XDM, XDM 3.8 (inch barrel) Compact and an XDS (subcompact).

Once we find a gun that fits we can worry about what type of ammunition it takes. These days most models of guns are available in different cartridge designations so when you find a fit you can then choose which cartridge you prefer.

Gun manufacturers make the same model of gun chambered for various cartridges. Smith and Wesson's Military & Police (M&P) line has a large variety of models and sizes chambered in .22LR to .45ACP. There really is something for just about everyone with this line and they are not the only company doing this. So chances are you can find a great gun to suit your needs; you just might need some patience. And if you are anything like me you may need to show great restraint, or you could end up with *a lot* of guns. There's nothing wrong with that, of course!

*Figure 6: M&P 9mm (top) and M&P .22LR
(bottom) both have the same size frame.*

Most people start with cartridge designation and go from there. I am not so much concerned with this as you can always learn to shoot a gun that fits you properly no matter what cartridge it shoots!

> **TIP:** If you narrow down your choices using the criteria above you might want to try and rent some or all of the guns on your "short list" and try them out before you buy. Many gun store/ranges have this option available to you. Renting different sized guns to find what you're most comfortable with is highly recommended.

AMMUNITION

What's the deal with all these different types of ammo anyway? There are three major hurdles with ammunition. (Many thanks to my husband, Jeff Meek, for coming up with the "Three Hurdles"; this makes it easier to explain and learn this material).

The first hurdle of ammunition is to know what kind of ammunition your gun shoots, and buy only that.

If you just bought this great 9mm pistol you need to buy 9mm ammunition. Sounds like a no brainer right? Well, did you know that some cartridges (the term referring to one round of ammunition as defined earlier) can have more than one designation? To keep

> **TIP:** There are four main components to a cartridge. They are the primer, (the part the firing pin hits) the powder charge (gunpowder), the case (holds all the parts together) and the bullet. When I refer to a 'bullet', I am referring to the part of the cartridge that is the projectile.

with the 9mm example, three very common names for 9mm cartridges are 9mm Luger, 9mm Para or Parabellum and 9x19 mm. The trick question I ask in class is "What is the difference between these cartridges"? The answer: there is *no* difference. They're all different names for the same thing. But, you have to know that! This same principle also holds true for .45 Auto and .45ACP, by the way.

By knowing what your gun shoots you will not have to rely on the guy behind the sporting goods counter at the discount department store to make the decision for you, or worse yet, lead you in the wrong direction when it comes to selecting *your* ammo.

TIP: *By law there are three places where the cartridge designation has to be identified. Those places are on the pistol itself (many gun manufacturers will stamp it right on the barrel), stamped on the cartridge case (head stamp) and printed on the factory ammunition box. This will help ensure that you are buying and using the correct ammo for the gun.*

Figure 7: Stamp of the barrel of a Glock Model 19.

Figure 9: Head Stamp on a Cartridge, this is a Speer Gold Dot in 9mm Luger.

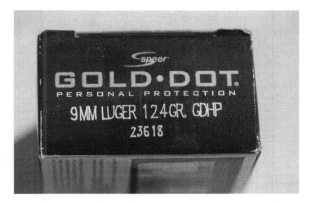

*Figure 10: Marking on the Ammunition box
for Speer Gold Dot 9mm Luger.*

The second hurdle of ammunition is the word "caliber". Most if not all modern firearm cartridges have a number as part of the name: .380 Auto, 40 S&W, .45ACP, etc. We all want that number to mean something. Then add that to this word "caliber" that we hear constantly, which has no direct bearing on any of this (but we want it to), and presto: we have an equation for disaster. We want so desperately for the number in the name to equal "caliber". But that's one level of extra work that we put into this that is completely unnecessary, at best. At worst, it could be catastrophic. Everything goes back to rule #1: what does my gun shoot? For example, if I own a 40 S&W, do I care if it's a "40 caliber?" Not even a little bit. But what I do care about is what my gun shoots. So if I learn the name 40 S&W, I can buy 40 S&W ammo, my gun runs it just fine, and everyone is happy. Stop trying to do math with words. Leave the "number equals caliber" equation to the other guy; skip that step completely. Learn what your gun shoots and forget the rest. It

> **TIP:** *The word "caliber" is a measurement of diameter only. In the case of ammunition it refers to the diameter of the bullet (projectile). It does not really matter what the diameter of our bullet is. Learning the name of the cartridge or the "cartridge designation" is your best bet to end up with the proper ammunition for your gun.*

would be helpful if they made color coded tags for guns and ammo that made a match when you got the right combination, just like that line of clothes did when we were kids. You always knew what went with what. Even my Dad could make a good looking outfit out of those, and that was a tall order!

The third hurdle of ammunition is +P and +P+ Ammunition.

Some ammunition has a +P or +P+ designation. The "p" stands for pressure. This indicates that the ammunition is loaded to higher than standard pressure for better or different ballistic performance. So if +P is more pressure than +P+ is even more pressure.

> **TIP:** +P and +P+ cartridges have the same dimensions as standard cartridges and can be chambered in guns that are not certified for higher pressure ammunition. Always use the proper ammunition for your gun.

The best analogy I can give you for this is to think of it as you would different grades of gasoline. There are usually regular, premium and super grades of gasoline available to us when we go to fill our gas tanks. The variances in grade refer to the octane levels in the gasoline. It's the same with ammunition. We have standard, super (+p) and super-duper (+p+) in terms of pressure.

This higher-pressure ammunition must only be used in a gun that is rated for use in this type of ammunition. This should be mentioned in the owner's manual that came with your gun. In some cases it could be marked on the gun itself. It should be noted that many of the sub-compact carry guns available today are not rated for the higher pressure +p or +p+ cartridges. If you are unsure if your gun is rated for this type of ammunition you should call the manufacturer and ask.

There are clear advantages and disadvantages to using higher pressure cartridges. Let's say that it's wintertime and people are all bundled up in layers of heavy clothing and parka, or for some strange reason you are hunting bear in Alaska (I know, this would be crazy). In both of these cases, +P or +P+ might be a really good thing to use to get through heavy layers of clothing that an attacker might be wearing or to penetrate dense bone and thick fur

On the other hand, over-penetration might be a concern if you live in an apartment and don't want the bullet to travel through a bunch of walls. A standard 9mm hollow point bullet can travel approximately 1100 feet/second. So, we'd better be able to hit our target and only our target! If we hit the bad guy, but the bullet goes through a bunch more walls and then hits a grandmother knitting in her apartment, we're going to jail.

Now that we have cleared the three main hurdles of ammunition, let's talk about the difference between practice ammo and self-defense ammo.

Practice ammo or range ammo goes by many different names; a couple of common names for it include round nose ammunition and full metal jacket (FMJ). This type of ammunition has a smooth surface, whether the bullet happens to be flat or round. The reason you don't want to use this for self-defense is it is known for passing through its intended target and hitting other unintended targets, as the bullet does not expand on impact. That's the down side, the upside is range ammo is usually less expensive than self-defense ammo. This should encourage you to buy some and get in some practice time!

Self-defense ammunition, commonly referred to as hollow point, does not have a smooth tip like round nose ammunition does. The hollow point bullet has a pit or hollowed out center in its tip. Hollow point ammunition is designed to rapidly expand upon impact. This rapid expansion creates drag and actually slows the bullet down upon impact with the target (think of putting on the brakes). This is important because this helps to keep the bullet from passing through the intended target and hitting an unintended target. Hollow points also create more destruction in the target. This is actually a good thing as it limits the amount of shots it will take to stop an attacker. For these reasons, hollow point ammunition is a better choice for self-defense or 'carry' ammo than FMJ ammunition. Self-defense ammo is more expensive, but the good news is that you will have to purchase less of it because (we hope!) you won't be shooting it regularly.

Figure 11: Bird's Eye view of different types of cartridges. Left to Right: Range Ammo (FMJ or Ball), Self-Defense (hollow point) and a hollow point with a polymer tip.

Figure 12: Side View of different types of cartridges. Left to Right: Range Ammo (FMJ or Ball), Self-Defense (hollow point) and a hollow point with a polymer tip.

Now that we have talked about buying a gun and choosing ammunition, I need to address this thing referred to as *Stopping Power*. Stopping power is one of the most highly debated and contentious subjects in gun culture.

It is highly recommended that once you decide on, or better yet, when you are in the process of deciding on a type and brand of self-defense ammo that you take it to the range and try shooting it in your gun. The reason this is important is because some guns are pickier than others and not all guns will be able to run all self-defense ammo. I would rather that you find this out early on rather than when it's too late. For example, neither one of my carry guns will run the brand of self-defense ammo that I originally chose. But once I figured this out, I was able to choose a brand/type that did work and I plan on sticking with it!

People like to tell you that any cartridge smaller than a .45ACP won't stop a bad guy. I actually couldn't disagree with that statement more. I carry a polymer frame gun chambered in 9mm. I chose this gun and cartridge because it is more pleasant for me to shoot and I can put more rounds on target, where I intend for those rounds to go, in a quicker time frame than if I chose to shoot something such as .45ACP. It's not that I *can't* shoot a subcompact .45ACP, but it is a lot less pleasant for me to shoot it than to shoot 9mm cartridges with a gun that is small enough to be comfortable for *me* to carry.

If you are proficient and confident with a gun chambered for .22LR then carry one of those. Trust me; you can protect yourself far better with a .22LR that you can hit your target with than the .45ACP that you are not able to shoot accurately or quickly. I can almost guarantee that if you needed to pull a weapon in the name of self-defense that your attacker won't stop and ask "Hey, what is that you're shooting?" More likely, they will run out of fear of your ability to neutralize the threat that they bring.

So, check your machismo at the door and find a cartridge that works for you, then get good at it. You'll thank me for this advice some day!

GUNS AND KIDS

Now that you have bought a gun and cleared the hurdles of ammunition you are set to bring your gun to its new home. Will the gun at any time be sharing a home with children? What about grandchildren from time to time? Whether that gun will be sharing a home with kids on a regular basis or for a few short hours or days, we still need to treat the guns the same way. Since I have a little guy in the house, I have some thoughts on this. I have a school-aged son so this is a topic that is near and dear to my heart.

Jeff and I started the process of teaching gun safety with our kiddo when he was about four years old, as he was at a good age and more importantly, a good maturity level to understand some of this stuff and be taught about the responsibility of guns. If we had started this any earlier than this age it would not have sunk in, in my opinion. All kids are different so age four might not be right for your family, but no one knows your child better than you. So follow your gut when it comes to teaching your child about guns. We started this process slowly. One day Jeff took apart a pistol so that it was on the table in several pieces, and he brought our son into the room and showed him the different parts and taught him what each part was. Then they cleaned the parts and put the pistol back together.

*Figure 13: Jeff and Kyle (Age 4ish) cleaning guns
together for the first time. Photo by Jenna Meek*

The next time they cleaned a gun together they started with an assembled gun and took it apart. The reason we chose this approach was so our son knew that even though this is a gun, it's also just a bunch of parts. It will also help when we teach him how this thing works as he'll already know what the parts are. Now we have a helper every time we clean guns. Often when we come home from time at the range we'll get "Hey, Mom and Dad do we have any firearms to clean?" If the answer is yes we'll hear "I want to clean the barrel!" This is his favorite part by far to clean. He's also gotten to the age that he will play DJ and turn on the iPod so that we have music while we clean guns. It has become quite the bonding experience!

The most important thing we can do as responsible gun owners is keep our guns secure. This means keeping them in a gun safe, and inaccessible to unauthorized persons. An unauthorized person is anyone who does not have permission to handle your gun. This can include, but is not limited to, people doing work in your home or guys from the cable company, kids and anyone else who comes into your home that you don't want handling your firearms. This also applies outside of the home. Our responsibility to keep our guns secure does not end when we leave the house, whether the gun is on our person or being safely left behind.

There are many different types of safes on the market today that are inexpensive and easy to use. Some can be mounted to a shelf in a closet, have biometric scanners and keypad entry. Most will also have a backup quick-open key that can be used. I don't care what kind of safe you use, so long as you use one! Safes have come a long way in the past few years and can be relatively inexpensive compared to the investment you've already made with a gun, so let's do it right and lock up those guns when we don't need them.

I personally tend to shy away from two types of safes: the safe that uses batteries to operate the door and the safe that uses a fingerprint scan to open the door. I am not crazy about battery-operated safes because the batteries will eventually die. Think of this like a smoke detector battery that always dies in the middle of the night and wakes you up. Yep, I have a safe like that! It never fails that the batteries die at 3 am and the notification beep wakes me out of a sound sleep. The worst part is that Jeff never hears it so I either have to wake him up to deal with it or get up and do it myself if I want to go back to sleep. If the batteries are dead and you don't know it, how long would it take you to get into that safe if you were in a hurry? Where do you keep the backup key? I also have used an older model safe with a fingerprint scanner. Maybe the technology has improved in the last few years, but I cannot get into that safe in a timely fashion. There is something about having to place your finger on the scanner in just the right way in order to open it that I just can't get right. Needless to say, I usually try three times, get locked out and have to wait about 15 minutes for the time delay to wear off to either try again with the fingerprint or get the backup key. Either way, this is a colossal pain in the neck. I no longer use this safe to store safety rescue equipment (Massad Ayoob's term, not mine) or for anything I might need to get to in a hurry!

Here is another thing about kids and guns. Most of the time kids get into trouble with their parents' (or other grownup's) guns because of curiosity. If we can take the element of curiosity away we've done a better job. This concept is written about by Massad Ayoob in "*Gun Proof Your Children*". For example, if my son ever wants to talk about guns, see a gun, or even hold a gun I will stop what I am doing and help to satisfy his curiosity by letting him see, touch or hold a gun in a safe manner. Just know that with this approach, your kids will always want to see a gun when you have approximately a million things going on. So be prepared to set everything aside and address the gun curiosity. You can pick up the million things right where you left them five minutes ago, they aren't going anywhere. The more I can teach my son about guns and gun safety in general, the less I have to worry about him trying to learn about them on his own. I am not worried about him with our guns. That said, they are still locked up. I am more worried about the guns that he might come across outside of our home. We may not know how guns are treated in the homes of others that we may visit.

> **TIP:** If you are in the market for a new safe get the biggest and best quality safe that you can afford at the time. This will be an excellent investment, especially if you plan to grow your gun collection at some point. I only wish I had thought of this before it was too late! One major safe manufacturer says the number one complaint they hear is "I should've bought a bigger size." Oh how true, especially if you get a good safe – you start finding more and more things worth locking up, even if they aren't more guns. Spend more than you want to and your future self will thank you.

The other thing we have taught our son is the *Eddie Eagle* program by the NRA. Eddie Eagle teaches kids that if they come across a gun and there is no adult around that they need to:

- ☞ Stop
- ☞ Don't Touch
- ☞ Run Away
- ☞ Tell a Grown-Up

My son teaches this concept in most of our classes as well as rules for safe gun handling. He started teaching the grownups when he was about four and a half years old. He used to do this while sitting at the back of the room. One day we put up a slide prompting our students to tell us what the rules for safe gun handling were, when all of a sudden our four and a half year old named the safety rules before any of our adult students did. This went on for a couple of months. Finally Jeff and I would ask the little guy if he wanted to tell the students what the rules were. One day when we asked him to do this he rose from his chair and sauntered to the front of the classroom (in a dramatic fashion, which he must get from his Dad). He then proceeded to hijack the class and "teach" the grown-ups the rules for safe gun handling. For a couple of years this was adorable!   Now that he is getting older, it's not as cute. But, I can think of nothing better to drive this point home than a young man who knows this stuff inside out, backwards and forwards. If he can learn this stuff and put it into practice then there is no reason that we can't do it too!   My kid also takes his job very seriously! One day he was very sick and it was early in the morning and we just happened to have a class that day. When I told him that he and I needed to stay home from class he was crushed. He was very concerned about how our students were going to learn the safety rules and *Eddie Eagle* without him. I had to reassure him that his Dad could handle it. He was skeptical, but it all worked out in the end.

If you are still having a hard time with this concept, let me throw something else out there for your consideration. We keep all kinds of potentially dangerous items in our homes. Most of these things are kept within reach of or in plain sight of our children; take, for example, kitchen knives. In our home, and millions of other homes, knives are kept in a knife block on the kitchen counter. Oh. My. Gosh. How could parents ever be so careless as to leave a deadly weapon accessible to their children?! We keep our knives out, but have taught our children from a very young age that these are a kitchen tool. They are sharp and if they are not used properly with the right

*Figure 14: Kyle (Age 6) helps Jeff teach the safety
rules to the grown-ups. Photo by Jenna Meek*

*Figure 15: Kyle and I clowning around at the
back of the classroom. Photo by Jenna Meek*

kind of care and respect, we could get hurt. Now, I am not saying there are no kitchen knife accidents involving children. Heck, the number of knife incidents in my house alone is in the double or triple digits, but that's all me and my clumsy self in the kitchen. Just ask my mom, I nearly stabbed her one time while she was trying to help out in my kitchen. I turned around from using the sink, knife in hand and was looking right into the face of my dear mother. She was right there and within striking distance. There was also the time that I dropped a chef's knife and it landed with the blade tip down and got stuck in my hardwood floor millimeters from my foot. That was a close call. To this day there is a small gouge in my wood floor from that incident. Jeff likes to point out that mark in the floor to me from time to time. In spite of these accidents, I am happy to report that there has never been a serious injury in my kitchen resulting from the use of a kitchen knife. Now, the mandolin slicer is another story and for my own safety, I no longer own one of those. We don't even need to talk about all the different ways we can burn ourselves in the kitchen, do we? Unfortunately, I know a thing or two about burns as well. For being so clumsy, it is a wonder that I have made it this long. Just to redeem myself a bit, I have been told that I am a good cook.

> **TIP:** If the topic of guns is treated matter-of-factly with your kids it will make a world of difference. Just now my son gave me a hug around the waist and touched the gun on my hip in the process. He didn't even bat an eyelash. This is pretty cool if you ask me! He is a very observant child; Jeff and I often joke that he's going to be an investigator of some kind when he grows up because he notices everything. I don't know if he didn't notice the gun or didn't know it was a gun, (which I would find hard to believe) but he wasn't curious about it – which is the point.

All I am saying here is that children can be responsible. It takes some work on our end, but it can be done. If this is something that you feel strongly about but is outside your comfort zone or you just aren't sure about how to do this, then I recommend getting in touch with a local instructor or a friend who is knowledgeable and ask them to sit down with you and your children and get the dialogue started. If you are in the greater Denver, CO area, then call me and I will make time to do this with you and your children. My little guy can help!

On-Body Carry

Now that you have made it this far, how and where are you going to carry this thing?!

When it comes to holsters, there is good news and bad news. First, the good news, there are a ton of holster options on the market today. Even better than that, the market for women's holsters has exploded (in a good way) over the past ten years or so. The bad news is that until we can figure out what options are best for us, we are going to kiss some frogs.

Jeff and I have drawers full of holsters that don't work or are not good quality products. Even men can have a tough time finding *the one* when it comes to holsters. In our case, there is one benefit to having a bunch of holsters lying around. We are able to bring them to class and let our students play with them to try and help them find a holster that might work for them. Now, when I get a not-so-great-for-me holster, I add it to the holster bag. I keep telling myself that I am conducting important research.

No matter how you carry a gun there is one piece of vital equipment (ok, two pieces of vital equipment) you have to have - a holster. I will go into detail about types of holsters in this chapter. I will also discuss how one may wish to go about choosing a holster. The second piece of equipment that I alluded to is a gun belt. I'll speak more about the gun belt later.

You might be wondering why a holster is so important. The number one, most important reason that we use a holster is for safety! Other important reasons to use a holster are for security of the firearm, consistency (of presentation and placement on your person or in your off-body carry bag, pack or purse) and comfort.

As stated above, safety is paramount. A holster keeps you safe, as a good holster will cover the trigger guard on the gun. This is important because the gun can't go bang unless we pull the trigger. If the trigger guard is not covered then it's not a safe holster.

I can illustrate this point for you. One day Jeff and I were out at the range with some friends, who were a married couple. The husband was wearing a beautiful, old leather belt holster with a full size 1911 in it. We asked him if there was a story behind the holster because we hadn't seen one quite like it before. As he turned to let us get a better look

TIP: Speaking of Safety and Security, I would be remiss if I did not mention the holster tip test. A good holster will keep your gun secure when tipped upside down. To test this place an unloaded gun into the holster and tip it over above a soft surface, such as your bed or couch. If the gun stays in while the holster is upside down, then the holster is considered to be safe.

at the holster Jeff noticed that the trigger guard of the gun was completely exposed. Wow! Although beautiful, this was the most unsafe holster we had ever seen. Here's the ironic part. The wife of the guy wearing the holster happened to be a police detective and she had never noticed that the trigger guard of her husband's gun was exposed. So the lesson here is pay attention and make sure you have a safe holster, please.

Security is another important reason to use a holster. Holsters will help keep the gun under your control. There are different types of retention tools on holsters. Some have a thumb break that goes around the back of the slide (not the frame of the gun) and holds it in the holster. To draw the gun the thumb break has to be unsecured first. Some holsters have retention screws that you can tighten to the right tension for your gun and other holsters have "buttons", for lack of a better term, that you have to press in order to draw your gun. In my opinion, these are not the best holsters out there. It can be easy to accidentally get your finger on the trigger while drawing your gun; this can lead to big, loud problems.

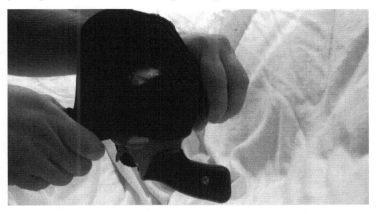

Figure 16: Jeff is pictured performing the tip test. The gun stays holstered while it is upside down. This is an example of a safe holster. Photo by Jenna Meek.

Consistency of presentation is another benefit that holsters offer us. Knowing exactly where your gun is when you need it, is what it is all about. If you wear your gun on your hip every day of your life, for example, and you practice getting to it, then your draw will be the same every time. This is great because you will know just how long it takes you to get to your gun and get rounds on target. This is true of any carry method you use. The key is to practice.

Comfort is also an important factor because if there is not a certain level of comfort it is highly likely that

TIP: We (Ladies) are likely to have many different carry options depending on what we are wearing, how we are feeling, where we are going, and so on. It is important to practice your draw stroke for all of the different carry methods you are interested in using! Knowing how to get to your gun when you need to and how long it takes to get it into the fight is imperative!

you won't actually carry your gun. Not all holsters will be 100% comfortable. I have heard people describe holsters as they would support wear. That is to say, you're happy to wear it all day, but are also happy when you can take it off at night. I think this is a good descriptor.

I need to tell you that choosing a holster or carry method can be difficult. Just as there are no perfect guns there are also no perfect holsters or way to carry. My shopping advice for holsters is the same as it is for guns. Find a holster or carry method that you can live with – including the drawbacks – and this will make life a little easier. Oh – and there is another consideration that I should bring to your attention when it comes to holsters. For me holsters are like shoes; I require many holsters and carry methods, depending on what I am wearing on any given day. The possibilities are nearly endless.

In the early days of my gun carrying journey, my husband's solution to my problem of finding a good carry method was to have me strap a holster to my hip and be done with it. How many of you have had a well-meaning man in your life tell you something similar? I thought so. Once I learned that just because it's right for my husband, or another important person in my life, it doesn't have to be right for me, I was much better off.

Realize that some holsters will require you to change the way you dress. Some will work well with how you dress every day, but won't work for formal wear. Some holsters can be very concealable and some are not so easy to conceal. It really depends on the person, the gun and the carry method. At this point you are probably wondering how to choose a holster. My advice is to consider the pros and cons of a holster and go with the one that has drawbacks that you can live with. This will go a long way to helping you have a good relationship with that new holster.

There are so many great alternative carry options available that with some perseverance, patience and practice, I am confident that you can find the perfect carry method for you, without having to completely change the way you dress! This is something that took me some time to figure out. I am always trying new methods; you just never know when something will come along and change your life!

I've included further information about holster types and the pros and cons for each type. The list of holsters I will discuss is not exhaustive, but these tend to be the most popular holster types that I field questions for.

Some common On-Body holster types include:

- Belt holsters
- IWB (inside the waistband)
- OWB (outside the waistband)
- Shoulder holsters (many variants available today)
- Ankle holsters
- Thigh holsters
- Belly bands
- Compression shorts and tank tops

There are many kinds of belt holsters available to us today. Some of the materials include but are not limited to:

- Leather
- Kydex ™
- Leather and Kydex ™hybrid
- Thermoplastic
- Nylon

Leather holsters are very comfortable for most people. A good leather holster will be nice and stiff and will hold your gun snugly. These holsters can be made for IWB or OWB. A quality leather holster should last you a number of years before needing to be replaced. Leather will wear out over time so you will have a good idea of when it is time to replace it. Leather as a holster material has been around for a long time. There are a bunch of reputable holster manufacturers using a variety of leathers. I've seen bull hide, horse hide, ostrich, stingray, and more. Read some reviews, and ask around for opinions; you can't go wrong with leather.

Figure 17: Leather (OWB), this is a Thrasos
by Soteria Leather.

TIP: *Sometimes leather holsters on leather belts can "squeak" when you move around. One thing that I have found helpful for this minor annoyance is to use a little baby powder or cornstarch on the holster. Do not soften either the belt or the holster with things such as leather conditioner or saddle soap as these are designed to soften the holster and this can harm the effectiveness of the holster and/or belt. Remember that they are stiff by design and we should keep the integrity of that design.*

Kydex ™is a high-tech, heavy-duty plastic material. These holsters are almost always custom made for your gun. The gun should fit snugly in the holster. There is sometimes a way to change the retention (how tight or how loosely the gun fits) of the holster. This is known as the amount of retention a holster has. One drawback to using a Kydex ™ holster is that when it gets worn out, it can break without warning.

Figure 18: Kydex ™ Paddle Holster (OWB)
by Comp-Tac.

The Hybrid Kydex ™/leather holster is also a popular option. Most of these have a leather backing (the part that is near your body) while the part that holds the gun is made of a Kydex ™ shell or "skin". The nice thing about some of these is that the skins may be able to be changed out to accommodate different firearms with one holster. The theory with the hybrid holster is that you can get the best of both worlds: the nice leather against your skin but the thinness and strength of Kydex ™ supporting the gun. It doesn't always work out that way, but that's the theory.

Figure 19: Hybrid
(Kydex ™/leather
OWB) by Comp-Tac.

Thermoplastic is also a hard plastic type of holster. Like Kydex ™, it will be made for your specific gun in order to make it work. It is not as heavy duty as Kydex ™ and is usually less expensive to purchase and to manufacture.

*Figure 20: Thermoplastic holster. This is the
Marilyn by Flashbang Holsters.
Photo by Jenna Meek.*

Nylon holsters are readily available in most gun stores and at gun shows locally. These are made in many different sizes to accommodate different sized guns. They are not usually custom made due to the nature of the material and the ease of switching between many different guns (so long as they are of similar size). I generally don't recommend the use of a nylon holster for everyday carry, as the quality is not as good as the leather and Kydex ™ holsters. One thing I really like to recommend the nylon holster for is to try out a new carry method now and then. This way you know if something will work for you with a minimal investment before you spend the time, energy and resources on a long term holster.

*Figure 21: Nylon IWB holster
(brand unknown).*

There are two main ways to carry a gun on your belt: Inside the Waistband (IWB) and Outside the Waistband (OWB).

Carrying a gun inside the waistband means that the gun is between your body and the waistband of your pants. The belt would then be attached to the holster via one of the methods I mentioned above. This is a very concealable way to carry. It is likely that you won't need a cover garment with an IWB holster. Sometimes a t- shirt is enough, depending on the style. I know several ladies (including myself most days now) who carry in an IWB holster and really like that method. Just remember to plan accordingly when you go shopping for pants and belts; they will likely need to be a bit or even significantly bigger to fit a holster and gun in them. I know it is a difficult concept, but now is not the time to get an ego about what size we wear. Buy what fits, not what should fit. For years the thought of carrying IWB was something I really hated, but as time goes on I have found this to be a more plausible option. It won't be right for everyone, but it is the most concealable way I have found to carry a gun on my belt.

*Figure 22: Kydex ™ holster worn in the Appendix
Inside the waistband (AIWB) position. Holster
by Custom Carry Concepts, LLC.*

Figure 23: AIWB holster shown concealed.

The other type of belt holster is worn outside the waistband. This holster attaches to your belt on the outside of the waistband of your pants. You will usually need a cover garment such as an over shirt, heavy sweater, vest or baggy t-shirt to successfully conceal a gun carried OWB. While this is not the easiest method of carry to conceal it is rather comfortable. Okay, let's be realistic: OWB is *way* more comfortable. That doesn't mean that IWB is, by definition, not comfortable. I'm just calling a spade a spade. I find that it is easier to pull off OWB carry in the winter when we wear heavier clothing.

Figure 24: Leather OWB behind the hip.

Figure 25: Leather OWB behind the hip shown concealed.

Whether you choose IWB or OWB carry, if you are going to carry a gun on your belt you have to have a belt designed for just this purpose! Gun belts are designed to be very stiff. This helps to distribute the weight of the gun and the holster (also called a rig) and keeps the rig from sagging or flopping around. Most gun belts are made from double thick leather and some may even be reinforced with Kydex ™. A well-made gun belt is vital to helping your holster do its job well. It's also likely that your belt will outlive your carry holster. Take care of it and you'll love it or many years. Please don't skimp on the belt!

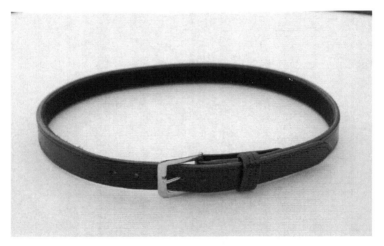

Figure 26: An example of a good sturdy gun belt. This belt is from The Beltman.

There are many positions for wearing a gun on your waist. These positions correlate to the positions on a clock dial. For instance 12 o'clock is at your belly button, 3 o'clock is on your right hip, 6 o'clock is at the small of the back (SOB) and 9 o'clock is on your left hip.

TIP: When it comes to carrying on your waist the position of the gun makes all the difference in the world. It's okay to experiment with the placement; in fact, I highly recommend it. It's tough for us ladies to carry on our hips. This is the widest part of our bodies and finding clothes to conceal a gun in this position and still be flattering is damn near impossible. Try moving the gun just behind your hip or in the appendix position instead. If you have already decided on your carry gear but can't make it work, experiment. Move things around and try again. Don't give up!

I happen to dislike – ok, I *hate* – wearing a belt, and remember how I just told you that the most important part of carrying on your waist is having a solid, stiff gun belt? I may have failed to mention that it should be worn tight enough to keep your gun from falling down. This makes it a little more unbearable for me to use a belt holster. Sigh.

Ankle holsters are another type of on-body carry holster. These serve a limited purpose, in my opinion. If you have a job where you are seated most of the day and you can easily bend down to get your gun, then an ankle holster might be for you. I don't think that they are useful when driving, as it is really hard

TIP: Look into different types of belts that can be more comfortable for women to wear. There are contour belts that have a subtle "u" shape that tend to fit curves better than straight belts; there are also tapered belts. Tapered belts are narrow in the front where they buckle and wider around the back. These help to have a more feminine look in the front while keeping strength in the back to help carry the weight of your rig.

to get to your ankle with a steering wheel in the way. They aren't the most comfortable holster out there and you cannot get to your gun while you are walking or running away from trouble. You will also not be able to get to a gun on your ankle if you are being attacked while on the ground (on your back, for example) and you will have to learn how to properly draw your weapon from an ankle holster. But don't count this carry method out; it's better than not having your gun at all. Just make sure you aren't trying to wear skinny jeans with an ankle holster as the profile can be bulky.

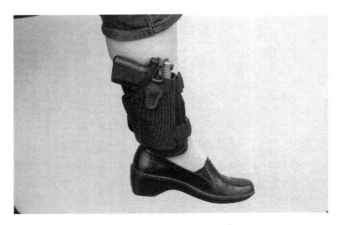

Figure 27: Shown here is an unknown brand of nylon ankle holster. Notice that the retention strap is not properly set up as a thumbbreak. This can cause problems with the draw. It may also be noted that this is a rather bulky holster.

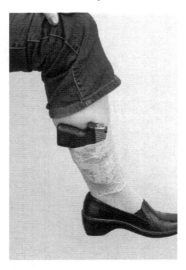

Figure 28: Shown in this photo is a low profile ankle holster by Femme Fatale. It is called the Ankle SoxXx.

Thigh holsters are great for use when wearing a dress or a skirt. These holsters are usually worn around the top part of the leg opposite your gun hand with the grip positioned on the inner part of the thigh so that it is easier to grip the gun while drawing. These can be a comfortable option for some ladies.

There are also shoulder holsters and shoulder holster variants. A shoulder holster keeps the gun under your arm on the weak side of your body. The weak side is the opposite side of the hand you shoot with. This is so that you can reach across your body with your strong hand to draw the sidearm. Shoulder holsters are not as common today as they were years ago. If you wear a jacket or blazer and never take it off then it could be a great option for you. There are also many variants of the shoulder holster that are becoming popular among women. These include, but are not limited to, bra holsters, kangaroo holsters, compression tops and belly bands if worn higher on the torso.

TIP: Contrary to popular belief, the size of your chest does not contribute to, nor inhibit your ability to safety draw from a shoulder holster or variant. There is a simple technique that makes it easy to draw. All you need to do is be able to give yourself a big hug. When you do this keep your off hand high (as in reaching over your strong side shoulder) and reach around your body with the hand that you are drawing the weapon with. This works to gain access to the weapon, which is actually worn on the weak side of the body when using a shoulder holster or shoulder holster variant.

Speaking of the good ol' bra holster; this has become a very popular option for women in the last few years. There are a few different bra holsters on the market. One of them is made of molded thermo-plastic and attaches to the front part of the bra with a strap and a strong directional snap. Once attached to the front of the bra, the holstered gun tucks up under the underwire of your bra. If positioned correctly the only part of the gun that is visible/accessible is the grip. This is so you can easily draw the gun. The same company that makes this holster also makes one that tucks into the side of the bra. It is secured with a strap around the side panel of the bra. It is designed to ride under your arm. These holsters tend to be easy to conceal. The comfort level is greater as the size of the gun decreases.

A belly band is a wide elastic "belt" with a Velcro or snap closure (I have even seen some with a hook and eye closure) and pockets sewn into it to accommodate your gun of choice. Some are made for smaller frame guns and some for larger frame guns. Belly bands can be made out of elastic type fabric or even out of neoprene. I have seen some that also incorporate lace for that feminine touch. Belly bands and belly band-type holsters can be positioned high or low on your torso, as well as in any position (think of the clock mentioned above) and can be worn IWB or OWB. If it is worn OWB you will need to have a good cover garment or heavy sweater as it is easy to make out the outline of the gun in a belly band. This is usually a great option for carrying as it is comfortable and no belt is needed.

One important thing to note with a bellyband: they should all have a retention strap or some sort of retention method! There is one company out there that makes a belly band-like product (don't call it a belly band, they don't like that) that is worn low on your hips. It has pockets all around for the gun to be worn in any position. The front pockets have magnetic retention (kind of cool!). I do think they need some kind of retention in the rear pockets, which they will do upon request. I actually have the retention magnets sewn into any pocket that I intend to carry my gun in and I also recommend the same to any one I tell about this holster. I like that added security. You don't want to go for a run and have your sidearm flopping around or wake up from a nap one day and find that your gun is on the loose. It can happen to even the best of us. The part about the nap is a true story told to me by a friend. I am withholding names to protect the innocent.

Figure 29: My go-to holster is a belly band type holster. Here it is shown being worn as AIWB. It also works for carrying behind the hip. This particular holster is the Classic Hip Hugger by Can Can Concealment

Figure 30: Can Can Concealment Classic Hip Hugger with a Glock 43. Photo by Jenna Meek.

In any case, no matter your shape or size there is a holster out there for you. Once you come to the conclusion that no holster is perfect, it will make your life easier. The trick here is to find a holster that has cons that you can live with. It's the same with guns, by the way.

I am always asked by my students "how do you carry"? My standard answer is "It depends on the day." or "What shoes am I wearing?" I will sometimes carry in a custom-made leather OWB holster and a sturdy gun belt at about 4 O'clock if I am wearing a big bulky sweater or a down vest as a cover garment. Alternatively, if it's on my waist it's in a belly band-type holster, or AIWB (Appendix inside the waistband) in a Kydex ™ holster.

TIP: *A proper thumb break is surprisingly hard to come by for some reason. With a thumb break there is a strap of some kind that goes around the back of the slide of the gun and is fastened on the inside part of the holster, closer to your body rather than on the outside part of the holster/gun. When you acquire your firing grip on the gun the motion of driving your thumb between the retention strap and the holster should break the retention. This is where the name thumb break comes from. You should be breaking retention with your thumb. Many of the retention straps that I see have the retention break on the opposite of the thumb side of the grip hand. This is a problem because it can take more time to draw your gun. Like everything else, we must practice this to become proficient.*

TIP: *Now that you know all about holsters, I should mention that not all EDC holsters are good for using on the range or in a class. If the holster is collapsible or you are physically unable to reholster your weapon one-handed, it is likely not going to be allowed by most reputable instructors. This can be a safety issue and since the job of the instructor is to keep you and your classmates safe, instructors will usually have a "recommended" holster list if you need some advice. All you have to do is ask! If you do have different holsters for use at the range and for EDC, then I absolutely recommend practicing with both of them so you can become proficient with all of your gear.*

OFF-BODY CARRY

Just as there are many different places to carry a gun on-body, there are many off-body carry methods as well. Please note that some of the methods we will talk about below can be considered on- or off-body depending on how they are worn (I have also heard these referred to as half-and-half holsters). For instance, if you wear a purse cross-body and never take if off then it could be considered an on-body carry method. This list is not exhaustive of carry methods; it is just enough to get you thinking creatively.

Off-Body Holsters:

- Day Timers

Half-and-Half Holsters (can be on- or off-body depending on how they are worn):

- Purse
- Fanny Packs
- Back Packs

Earlier in this book I mentioned that I am not a huge fan of carrying a gun in a purse, or in any other off-body carry method, for that matter. "Why is that?" you must be wondering. Ok, well here it comes. Before we delve into this topic, I should point out, as it was pointed out to me by Kathy Jackson (and I agree with this whole heartedly), that every woman who carries a gun should have a CCW purse as a backup method in the event of a wardrobe malfunction. So go ahead and get yourself a nice back up carry purse. Keeping this in your car in the event that you don't want to use it all the time is a great idea so it will be available to you if you ever find yourself needing another option when you are out and about.

Now, my reasons for shying away from off-body carry. If you are going to make sure your purse, fanny pack, or back pack never leaves your body, then this is a moot point. But most people don't do it this way so I feel that this is worth talking about. Let me start by asking you some questions to illustrate my point. When I use the word "purse" please note that it is interchangeable for fanny packs, day timers, backpacks etc…

- ☞ When you leave your house and you get in the car to go someplace, where do you set your purse?
- ☞ When you go to a friend's house what do you do with your purse?
- ☞ When you get to work what do you do with your purse?

If your answers are similar to those below, we have a problem:

TIP: *If you are going to purchase a gun purse I recommend looking for one made specifically for this purpose. Gun purses will have an easy access compartment with a built in holster to make the draw as quick as possible. They are also made with the safety of the firearm in mind. The other nice thing is that gun purses come in many fabric and style choices these days so it is likely that you will be able to find one that suits your taste.*

- ☞ I set it on the passenger's seat.
- ☞ I set it by the front door (or insert another place in the house that is not on your person, here) when I enter the house.
- ☞ I keep it in an unlocked drawer of my desk, which is located in a cubicle.

If you set your purse (containing a gun) down **anywhere**, you have also set your **gun** down! If we have set our gun down, it is no longer under our control and could become accessible to unauthorized persons. Our responsibility to keep that gun safe and in our control does not end when the purse or other off-body holster is set down.

There have been several stories in the news recently that illustrate this point for me. There is no question that the following events were sad and tragic. They are being used as an illustration of what can happen if we fail to be responsible.

In December 2014 an Idaho woman was accidently shot and killed by her two-year-old child. The child got the mother's gun out of her unattended purse while he was sitting in a shopping cart. In this case, the purse the gun was in was specifically designed as a concealed carry purse and it was given to the victim just prior to the incident as a Christmas gift, according to one family member. It appears that the victim was trying to be safe by using the proper equipment intended for the concealed carry of a firearm. Unfortunately, she fell short of being safe when she set the purse down where her child could gain access to it.

In another event from January 2015 a father and a pregnant woman were shot by a three-year-old boy in a motel room in New Mexico. The shooting happened when the toddler got a loaded gun out of the woman's purse. The father was hit in the lower back by his three-year-old son. The bullet went through his hip and struck the pregnant woman in the shoulder. In addition to the three-year-old boy there was a two-year-old girl in the room. The children were not hurt in the incident and thankfully the parents were also expected to be all right.

I can't stress this enough. You have to be in control of your weapon at all times!

The other reason purse carry can be a bad idea, is if something were to happen and you *needed* your gun, when your purse is on the passenger's seat, by the front door or in a desk drawer, or even draped over your shoulder. You now have to get to it and that might not be the easiest or quickest task to accomplish. Couple this with "OMG, he came out of nowhere!" and having your gun in a purse that you can't even reach normally, let alone when a bad guy is grabbing you, is a recipe for disaster.

I am also leery of purse carry because kids (or maybe husbands) always want to go into your purse to get something.

We have a rule in our house (well, lots of rules, but I am thinking of a specific one): no going in Mom's purse, for any reason, unless you have been given express permission to do so! Now, I *never* have a gun in an unattended purse, but you just never know who might. Does Grandma or a favorite aunt or friend carry in her purse and does Grandma, a favorite aunt or friend also let little Johnny go through her purse, for example? I make a point to teach my son not only to leave my purse alone, but to leave all purses alone. You just never know when there might be something in a purse. Maybe it's not a gun but it would still be unpleasant to find, for example, pepper spray, and find out the hard way what that is all about.

With purse carry or any other off-body carry method your gun becomes very difficult to get to if you need it. And the chances are if you need it, you are going to need it in a hurry.

If you must carry a gun in your purse, you must remember the following:

You have to keep the gun in its own separate compartment. There can be nothing but the gun in this compartment. This is for safety reasons and to ensure that you know where the gun will be if and when you need to get to it. It would be a disaster to reach in and grab sunglasses, for example, when you were in a hurry to get to your gun.

You have to keep the gun in some kind of a holster, and the holster must cover the trigger guard completely. It is not a holster if it doesn't cover the trigger guard. Even if the gun is in its own separate compartment all alone, it *must* also be in a holster and that holster *must* completely cover the trigger guard. Again, this is for safety. It would be tragic and negligent if a tube of lipstick somehow got wedged into the trigger guard and you moved the purse in just the right way to create enough force for the lipstick to pull the trigger and make the gun go bang.

You have to practice your draw. I can guarantee that it is going to take some work to get your gun out and get rounds on target from a purse. Trust me, I have tried this and just recently had a friend at the range and helped her practice this as well.

She was very surprised at how difficult this task was. She also had a hard time keeping the purse "stable" as she drew the gun. We have to account for this as well. We need to consider how we carry our purse. Is it always on our shoulder the same way, facing the same direction, do we sometimes carry it in the crook of our arm, is it always on the same arm? Do we shift our purse based on what we are doing or carrying at the time? Do we always carry the same exact purse or do we switch purses and use different styles of purses? I could go on and on, but I think you get my drift.

With all this talk about where and how to carry a gun, I need to make one thing clear. I don't particularly care what carry method(s) you decide on. This is a very personal choice. My hope is that I can give you the information that you need to make the best decision for yourself.

If you do decide that carrying in a purse (or off-body) is right for you, then you are one step closer to having your gun available to you should the need ever arise. I'll take that over leaving the gun at home any day of the week!

The thing I care about most is that you practice, practice and then practice some more on getting your gun out of concealment and getting rounds on target. I also don't care how long it takes you to get your gun out and get rounds on target. I do care that you know how long it takes and that you are prepared to use the appropriate tactics to give yourself the time necessary to properly defend yourself if it ever comes to that. This is important because contrary to popular belief, you cannot "just shoot through a purse".

> **TIP:** Most indoor ranges won't let you draw from a purse. Regardless of whether this is your primary carry method or not, however, you need to have done this with live fire under supervision at the range. There are a lot of moving parts (read: elbows) that can easily cover the muzzle. So don't shoot yourself, please. But you do need to have practiced this for real at the range, just like every other carry method. My advice is to find an outdoor range where this activity is permitted, or an instructor or a class for practicing with a purse since this activity is severely restricted in non-class settings.

Friends of mine at a well-known firearms academy have tested this "shoot through the purse" theory and the results were not favorable. It turns out that you are not at all likely to hit your target while shooting through a purse. On top of that, there are all kinds of things in a purse that can get in the way of the bullet on its way out. The testers found that the shots were nowhere near their intended targets when shooting though the test purses. There is also the factor of semi-automatic guns not properly cycling thus leading to jams. Revolvers had the same issue. The cylinders were getting caught on the lining of the purses, rendering the guns useless after one shot was fired. So at best, you may get one decent shot off – but it's highly unlikely you'll get two shots off. And I'm not sure what your accuracy is like when you shoot from the hip (not using your sights at all), but add in one-handed, a likely unconventional shooting position to begin with, a likely you have a poor grip, and God knows whatever else…and your odds of making a reasonable shot, even at close range, is somewhere between extremely unlikely and never gonna happen.

The other major issue that the testers discovered was that by the time they detected a threat and got the gun out of the purse and into the fight, it was already too late. The assailants had gotten to them first. Fishing a weapon out of your purse takes a lot of time, even when you know exactly where it will be and that there is a threat coming. Imagine how long it could take you to get your gun into the fight under the stress of a surprise attack.

Another thing about carrying in a purse that scares me is the violent crime of purse-snatching. Yes, I called purse-snatching a violent crime. Have you ever seen videos of these incidents? They are not usually quick and painless or friendly. Many times women are being shoved to the ground, stomped on or being attacked with fists or other weapons while the assailants are trying to get the purse from them. One of the worst purse-snatching videos I have seen was of a woman being dragged by a moving vehicle. The assailants never even got out of the car. They drove up alongside an unsuspecting woman and grabbed her purse strap and drove off. This lasts as long as she resists or the strap of the purse breaks and the criminals can take off. It takes seconds for this to happen.

Most women will fight over their purse. This could become especially true if it is holding a gun. The last thing I would want to willingly give to a bad guy is my gun! How about you? This is where I think the line has to be drawn on this topic. Would you risk your life to save your gun or your purse?

My friend, Don Stahlnecker of the Firearms Academy of Seattle, makes the analogy that your firearm is your bodyguard. Your bodyguard will dutifully sacrifice his life for yours. Let your gun do the same. Do *not* risk your life to save your gun. I know it sounds counter-intuitive for many, but let it go and just get the heck out of dodge.

TIP: We often refer to purse-snatchers as being male. But did you know that there are plenty of women out there who are partaking in this type of crime as well? A couple of reasons for this might be that there are not many people who suspect women of stealing purses and when a woman steals a purse and is walking down the street with it she does not look out of place because it is normal for women to carry a purse.

This brings us to what to look for in a CCW purse. These purses should all have a separate compartment to keep the gun and only the gun in. It should also have a nice big access to that compartment, big enough to easily get your gun out. I have seen these compartments secured with snaps, zippers, Velcro and more. In my opinion it doesn't really matter, so long as it keeps the compartment closed when it is supposed to and it is easy enough to open when it has to be.

These purses should have a holster. Some of my favorites come with Velcro attached in the compartment and have Velcro on the holster so that you can position the holster just right for your gun and the way you will access the gun for the draw. This holster doesn't have to be anything super fancy, it just has to keep the gun secure and keep the trigger guard covered. These holsters are usually a "one-size fits most" soft type of material or even nylon. That is fine, so long as it does its job, which again is to keep the gun in one place and cover the trigger guard.

Concealed carry purses should have a good sturdy strap that will help distribute the weight of the gun. Trust me, if you wear this the entire time you are out of the house, as I do if I happen to be carrying in a purse, they get heavy, fast! My gun alone weighs one and a half pounds, loaded. Add the weight of a holster and a full purse and you could be carrying 10 pounds of stuff easily, depending on what you keep in your purse

Now, a little bit about purse straps. I would be remiss if I did not mention the two schools of thought on the reinforced purse strap. The reinforced purse strap is usually seen more often on a purse that is worn cross-body style. But it is certainly not limited to this style of purse strap. The reinforced strap will usually have a heavy duty cable that is sewn into the nylon or leather purse strap, or it can be a chain-type strap (more on that shortly).

Some people are big fans of the reinforced strap. The rationale behind this is that if a mugger tries to cut the strap with a knife to steal it from you, they won't be able to. Those who oppose it believe that if you are wearing a reinforced strap purse cross-body style and a mugger attempts to cut the strap with a knife it puts you in danger, as the knife is likely to come into contact with your body and injure you in the process.

My opinion is to forego the reinforced strap if possible and let the purse go. Remember the bodyguard analogy?

I have seen some really pretty and well-made carry purses on the market recently that do not meet the criteria for a carry purse that I just listed above. My intent is to help inform more ladies of what to look for so that when you find that perfect gun purse you will know if it is as functional as it is pretty. Now if only my favorite purse manufacturer would make a carry purse I'd be in heaven. Maybe I'll work on that someday.

OPEN CARRY

Now that we have talked about carrying a concealed weapon, I feel like I should address the issue of open carry. For those of you who are wondering, "open carry" means to carry a gun in such a manner that anyone can see it. Students always want to talk about this. I will preface this by telling you that my reasons for not being keen on open carry have nothing to do with the fact that I teach concealed carry classes for a living. I will also tell you that if you are going to consider open carry that you need to be well-versed on the laws associated with this where you live. This legal thing, by the way, also holds true for concealed carry and owning and using guns in general. People, you *must* know the laws concerning these things. This is important because even though we may have the right to own and carry our weapons with us, some municipalities are allowed to make their own laws and part of being a responsible gun owner is following those laws. We'll dive into legal issues in a later chapter.

The decision to open carry or not is a personal thing, as so many decisions around choosing and owning a gun are. No one can tell you if it is right for you to do or not to do. I have decided that it doesn't make sense for me at this time. Who knows what my tastes will be in a year, or 10 years? That's why we fight for the right to do so: just because you don't have a good reason to do something doesn't mean you should remove that right from everyone. Please do your research and make an informed decision that works for you!

Here are my reasons for not being keen on the idea of open carry:

As I mentioned, if you are going to own guns then you need to know what the laws are where you live. This is especially true if you open carry. There are many cities and towns here in Colorado where it is perfectly legal to open carry, but if you go to a neighboring city or town, it may not be. It is not just your responsibility to know these laws, it's your obligation. You *must* be an expert!   This is vital, as in some states cities and towns can make their own laws regarding such things as the open carry of firearms.

Open carrying a gun *could* make the gun a target for thieves. Let's say you carry a full size gun (since it does not have to be concealed, that's what I would carry) and someone walks over and sees it; maybe that person just happens to really love your gun, and decides that they would like to try and take it from you so they can have it for themselves. By carrying a gun in plain view you have made it a target for crime. Now, is this likely to happen? I hope not, but sometimes people can get desperate and do things that they wouldn't ordinarily do, so in my opinion, let's not take that chance. On the flip side, there are plenty of Open Carry groups that would disagree with my opinion. Lots of open carriers argue that the act of open carrying actually deters crime. This is usually from the perspective of "if a bad guy sees a gun he's less likely to mess with that person". In some cases I think this is true. In other cases, not so much. Again, my stance on this is that I don't want to advertise anything that could potentially increase my threat profile.

The act of open carry may, in fact, unwillingly volunteer you for service. Let's say that you are open carrying and you happen to be in your local diner having breakfast with your family when a robber walks in and decides to demand money from the cashier stand. At that moment you decide that you will wait and see how this unfolds before you choose to act.

Let's face it, if he just wants cash and isn't going to hurt anyone, it may be best to let him take the money and be on his way. But in the middle of your act of watching the events unfold with a cautiously optimistic outlook, the person at next table, who can see your gun in plain view, suddenly decides to not so quietly urge you to stop the robbery in progress. Now, what may have been a quick in-and-out robbery might turn into a situation where you have been unwillingly volunteered to act.

Open carry takes away any tactical advantage you might have in carrying a gun. Let's say that you are armed and a bad guy decides to target you for a crime. If your gun is concealed you can play this any way you want, only revealing that you are armed if and when the time is right. However, if the bad guy knows that you are armed ahead of time he will be able to change his plans, which in turn could render your sidearm ineffective. If you're targeted for a crime based on other reasons than having the gun in the first place (point number 2 above), they're going to try and neutralize your weapon *first*. If they don't know it's there, you're dealing with a very different attack – and frankly, one that could be more survivable.

Given the political climate in our world today we must be very careful when we decide to carry a gun in the open. Be it right, wrong, or indifferent, when the general public sees a person walking around with a gun in plain view it tends to make many of those people very uncomfortable. This is especially true in Colorado (where I live) in the post Aurora Theater shooting era. People also use the argument of "Don't scare my children with the open carry of a gun". Ugh. While I think this is a ridiculous argument, I don't have the time or patience to try and reason with people when they try to express the dislike of seeing a gun in the open. I simply feel that keeping the gun concealed is an easier option. Also, if you should choose to open carry, please set aside a reasonable amount of time so you are able to have that friendly chat with your local police, as I am relatively certain that this will happen if you decide to carry a gun in plain view. If and when the boys in blue show up for that chat, please pass the "personality test" as my friend, Marc MacYoung, would say – although he would say it more colorfully than that. What I mean by "pass the personality test" is that spouting off to the cops that you are open carrying because it's within your rights as a citizen is not the best approach. The best way to pass a personality test is to be polite and calmly and rationally explain why you choose to open carry. If you are being responsible in your actions of openly carrying a weapon and your words match those actions, there should not be any further issue in dealing with the police.

In some states there could also be legal ramifications to open carry, based on some recent laws that have been adopted (yes, Colorado, I am referring to you) so you also want to make sure that you are familiar with any pertinent legislation that could impact you in a negative way should you decide to open carry.

There may be a time when people choose to open carry due to physical limitations. For example, I have a friend who is wheelchair bound. He does not have a good way to conceal a firearm that makes it readily accessible. Open carry makes perfect sense for him. He is able to have a gun for self-defense and it's easy and quick for him to get to.

Other people may choose to open carry because they don't want to go through the process to get a concealed carry permit. In my state it costs up to $152.50 and can take three months for your permit to be issued. There is also the time it takes to go apply for the permit in person that could prohibitive to some people.

On the plus side, open carry is often faster in drawing and deploying the weapon in a crisis than many concealed methods. This can be very important if you've found yourself being stalked by violent person intent on harming you.

If you should decide that open carry is right for you then please, please, please use a good and safe holster. This should be something sturdy and should also have some type of retention. This is important in the event that someone wants to target your gun, so that they will not be able to quickly slip it out of your holster. You should also be well-versed in handgun retention tactics as well. It would be a bad day for you if your gun were to ever be taken from you.

CARRYING IN THE HOME

It's a great idea to carry while you are at home. I know what you are thinking: "I am safe in my home with no perceived threats of violence. Why would I ever need to have my gun on me at home? " There are a number of reasons.

The first reason to carry at home is because your gun is safest when it's on your person. This is especially true if you have children of the curious kind. When my gun is on my person this is the only place that I know 100% without a doubt that no one is messing with it.

The second reason is in the event of a home invasion. Over the course of a couple of years I have heard more and more about daytime break-ins in the metropolitan area where I live. This has likely been driven by a downward economy. Thieves are getting desperate to make a buck and they figure that since people are at work during the day that they will just break into what they think are unoccupied homes, rather than break into homes at night when there is a better chance of people being around. Crooks are also getting sophisticated and bold. The way this usually goes is that they knock on the front door or ring the doorbell; if no one answers, then they find a way to get inside. Well, we (and half of the people on our street, for that matter) are home all day long. I also don't answer my door if I don't know the person who is knocking on the door. It's just not a good idea to be opening your door to strangers. It also helps me to not feel guilty for not wanting to buy what they are selling or to convert to their awesome religion.

One day I had the pleasure of answering the door to a uniformed police officer in the middle of the morning. It seems as though someone tried to break into a house on our street while the lady of the house was home. The police were notifying people on the street of what was happening and telling us to be cautious and to make sure our doors and windows were locked. Since I was already armed, I politely thanked the police officer and went about my business. I did not need to make changes to my security plan other than being aware that there had been an incident on my street and to pay a little more attention that day. It can be a strange feeling to have a conversation with the cops when you're packing heat and they don't know it.

It's not just daytime break-ins that we need to consider, either. If you were sitting comfortably on your couch one evening watching your favorite TV show and a bad guy crashed through your front door how long would it take you to get your gun into the action if you needed it? Test that theory sometime and get back to me. Unless you have a safe as a side table, it's probably going to take several minutes. Not only that, but is your gun in a location that you can safely get to without the bad guy seeing you while you rush for it? We often watch a TV show that chronicles actual survival stories of real people who have been victims of crimes and natural disasters. The stories are told by the survivors. One of the things I take away from that show is how many times people are attacked in their own homes and are completely defenseless against their attackers. I can say with certainty that if more of the victims had been armed at the time of these attacks, we'd probably be hearing a different story – or maybe not hearing about it at all.

Do you ever answer your door to strangers? I try not to, but sometimes it happens. One Saturday afternoon I was at home and the doorbell rang. For some odd reason I opened the door, when I wouldn't normally. Standing on my doorstep was a guy, probably in his early 20's, wearing a polo shirt and chinos. He was carrying a clipboard. He told me he was with a satellite TV company and asked me if we needed our satellite dish serviced. I thought this was strange. I politely told him no thanks, and closed the door. At that point I picked up the phone and called our satellite TV provider and asked if they had anyone in the area of my house working on satellite dishes. They said that they did not and that they would only ever send someone out if the homeowner were to request service. They then told me to call the police and report this, which I did. My bigger concern about this was for everyone else whose door he was going to knock on that day. I have no idea what he was up to, but I was smart enough not to give him the time of day. Too bad I wasn't smart enough to not answer the door in the first place. Looking back, this could have gone wrong in a hurry! Luckily nothing bad happened. It seems to me that the best way to gain entry into a home is through an open front door. If I had been the type of victim the guy had been looking for, maybe he would have forced his way into my home. Or maybe he just wanted to see the layout of my home and see who was around. I think that against an unsuspecting occupant, this ruse could be very effective.

Have you ever sold anything on an internet "classifieds" site and had to have people come check out your stuff, at your home? I don't use these resources often, but when I do have people come to the house, I am armed. It's just good practice. You already know that you have something that they want, but do you know if they are nice, respectable, upstanding citizens or not? I love giving people the benefit of the doubt, but I would be naive not to think that something had the possibility of going wrong, and if I wasn't prepared to take care of myself or the rest of my family that would make for a bad day.

How about having people doing work in your home? We recently had some work done at our house. I had three strangers (all male) in and out of the house all day long. My child was also home when they were here. So needless to say, I felt much better knowing that Jeff and I were equipped with the tools that we needed to defend ourselves and our son if something were to go terribly wrong. Best practice when you have to have people in your house to repair something is to "trust but verify".

A stranger is never allowed unescorted access throughout our home. We close doors to rooms not needed and lock them whenever possible. Also, besides keeping an eye on them, you can also learn some tips and tricks about maintaining your home by asking some questions. Simple things like "Wow, it sure was nice of you guys to make it out here on short notice" or "You're good at this – how long have you been doing this job? " tend to make them feel appreciated, and they're more likely to do a bang-up job in a shorter amount of time. That's a win-win.

You are also more vulnerable when you are in your home. What I mean by this is that we don't usually walk around our homes on high alert, paying special attention to everything going on around us. We don't have to because we are reasonably sure that if our doors are locked we will be safe. So think about the times during your day, while you are at home, that you are the most vulnerable. For me it's when I am distracted. There are many distractions in our homes. These can include: talking on the phone, checking email, watching TV, cooking dinner, taking a shower (no, I don't think that 'normal' people need shower guns, but it does make me chuckle. I mean, what are some people into that they would need to keep a shower gun?), coming and going from our homes, or even putting the kids to bed at night. If you always have your gun on you then you are prepared to deal with mayhem no matter when it strikes.

Now, I know what you are thinking... "She's crazy, carrying a gun is uncomfortable enough when I am away from home, now she's telling me I have to wear it *at* home too?!". I am not telling you to do anything you are not comfortable with; I am simply giving you the information that you need to make your own informed decision, in order to do what is best for you. Much of what I do as a firearms instructor is to arm people (no pun intended, I promise) with information and let them adapt their own routines and come to their own conclusions with regards to what best fits their lifestyles. Do I *always* carry at home? No. I wish I could say that I did, but when I am not carrying at home, I always know where the nearest gun is and what my route would be to get to it if I needed it in a hurry. I will say that if having a gun on your person becomes part of your lifestyle, then it gets harder and harder to not wear your gun most all of the time, even at home.

CARRYING IN PUBLIC FOR THE FIRST TIME

Now that you are ready to carry your gun outside of the home, I have some thoughts and observations about carrying in public for the first time. The first thing that I want you to know is that it is completely normal to feel self-conscious when going out in public for the first time with a concealed handgun. For Jeff and I, the first time we carried in public was at our local discount department store. For us this felt like a rite of passage. We specifically chose this place to test out our new skills as it was a good place to wear whatever we felt comfortable in. For me, that was an oversized sweatshirt and jeans. My thought process on this was, "There is no way I will print [see Tip, below] while wearing this, and since this is a casual environment I will not stand out as looking sloppy, especially compared to the people in pajama pants and slippers". I was almost overdressed in my big baggy sweatshirt. Who knew?

TIP: Printing is when the outline of your gun becomes visible through your clothing. Although not a crime in the state of Colorado where I live, the point is that you don't want people to know that you are carrying, and printing will give you away. As always, know your local laws. Printing in some states *is* against the law.

So, as I am walking through the store, I was stopped by a parent of one of my son's classmates, of all people, standing right there in the aisle between the big boys' clothes and the baby clothes. All I could think was "Great, I am busted"! I think I even started to sweat. Remember, at one time in my life I was a "closet" gun owner. Well, this encounter was during that time in my life. I politely made small talk and went on my way when the conversation ended. To this day, I don't think that other mom knew my secret. It's funny how your perspective changes, because today people who know me probably just assume I am armed and would be surprised if I wasn't, especially at said discount department store.

It is important to know that it is completely normal to feel like everyone is staring at you when you walk out of your home for the first time carrying a concealed handgun. We also tend to have specific behaviors while getting used to gun carrying as well. Some examples of this include: dressing in unseasonable clothing to have better cover garments, such as wearing a jacket in the summer when it's hot outside; keeping a hand on the gun while in the rain to attempt to keep the gun dry; brushing a hand or arm over the gun while walking, as if to make sure it's still there; and gun toters also tend to adjust their rig while getting into and out of their vehicles. Many gun carriers will do the readjust thing before the car door is even closed. I've spotted people carrying this way – not because I saw the gun or the outline, but because they just had to mess with it.

The good news about this is that people in general are oblivious to the things going on around them and unless they know what to look for in the way of a concealed weapon, they will never in a million years make you as carrying a gun. The only people who *might* notice your concealed weapon are those who also carry weapons, as they know what to look for. If it is well concealed, this shouldn't be much of an issue for you. Often times even people who carry concealed on a regular basis won't notice if and when you are carrying. It is pretty rare for me to notice if someone else is carrying, and teaching them how to do so is my job, so I am also pretty good at knowing what to look for. If I notice the gun, it is likely that I have inside information about that person to begin with. One other thing to note is that if a person with a concealed weapon does figure out that I am armed I don't much care, as we're on the same team, as it were.

The first time I met Kathy Jackson in person, I could not for the life of me figure out where her gun was, and we spent the whole day together with me looking her over. If she noticed my strange behavior, she did not let on. I was certain she was carrying, but I had no clue where it was. Just as I was conceding that maybe she had come unarmed, I summoned up the courage to ask if she was carrying. She said she was, told me where it was and in what type of holster. I went out and got one of those holsters right away. That was impressive to me. I don't think I offended her by asking – at least I hope not. Either way, I don't think she held it against me.

TIP: These behaviors will usually fade as you get more and more comfortable carrying. Just know that this happens to the best of us in the beginning, and as I mentioned, it's completely normal. Stick with it and you'll settle in soon enough!

Now that I have mentioned some pitfalls to that first time carrying in public, I want to tell you that you can get to the point where carrying a gun becomes second nature. I don't mean that you will lose respect for the gun or the responsibility that comes with owning it. I do mean that you will become comfortable with having that gun on you when you wear it. I have been carrying a gun for several years; I just had to renew my permit (it is good for five years) last summer, if that gives you an idea. In all these years of carrying I have gained confidence and have gotten rather good at concealment. When I first started to carry Jeff always knew where my gun was. Within the last year or so Jeff has started asking me if I am carrying when we go to leave the house. I take this as a compliment because he is not asking for the fun of it. I have gotten so good at concealing my weapon that he has resorted to having to ask me if I am armed because he can't tell. Woo hoo! I guess I have arrived. I am just sorry it took so many years to get up to speed. You should see the collection of holsters that I have amassed to get to this point.

THE OPINION OF FRIENDS AND FAMILY

Before Jeff and I started a firearms training company we were very 'hush, hush' about our gun lifestyle. We were afraid of what other parents from school would think of us, for example. Instead of telling them we spent the whole time shooting at the range when asked what we did over the weekend, we would say that we spent time with friends and enjoyed some fresh air. Well, gunpowder and lead don't exactly make for fresh air, but you know what I mean.

Now that the proverbial cat is out of the bag and we tell people what we really do in our spare time (especially as it's also our chosen line of work), we've been enlightened. Most people are supportive and are even interested in shooting or learning to shoot. It's opened doors for us and helped us to make some great new like-minded friends. I would not go back to living in the "gun closet" for anything.

I guess the bottom line is: don't worry what others will think about all this. It's your business and you can share it with others or keep it to yourself. It doesn't have to be a secret unless you want it to be. Embrace your gun ownership and enjoy knowing that you will have the tools you need help to protect yourself from violent crime if you ever have to.

It happens almost weekly that someone asks what I do for work. I know that the answer I provide will make the conversation go one of two ways; there is really no in-between.

The other person will either be very interested in the fact that I am a firearms instructor and want to talk about it for hours, or they will be appalled that I like guns. I have examples of both of these reactions.

In my son's old school (before the homeschooling days) each family was required to volunteer for a certain number of hours per school year. We were falling behind in our obligation, so I had the bright idea to offer to hold a class for the teachers and administrators as part of our volunteer time. I would say this was a very successful idea. The administration and the board met and talked it over and we were allowed to hold the class. We had the school principal and vice principal in attendance along with about a dozen other teachers. After the class, I had teachers approach me in the halls of the school (or in one case, I had a teacher ask me about training in a supply closet. No joke, an actual supply closet. She was so cute about it.) to whisper to me about their interest in getting training, but they didn't want their co-workers knowing about it. I was happy that these individuals trusted me enough to start the dialogue. Not only did we have teachers take a class, but we had parents on some of the school committees also take classes. I think that once you find out that these regular Joes are into guns and self-defense, it opens doors to others to reach their goals when it comes to the subject.

On the flip side, there was the time when I was talking to the mom of a classmate of my son and she asked me what I did for work (as that is always the ice-breaker question; maybe it is time to start getting creative with the ice-breakers!) and I told her. She replied that she was an Assistant District Attorney. That was the extent of our conversation. I don't know if it had to do with her work, or if she thought we were destined to meet up some day in the courtroom. Or it could be that she just hates guns. I am not really sure. But this pretty much sums up how fast this subject can kill a conversation. I still see this parent occasionally and she won't even acknowledge my existence.

I also have a friend who hates guns and is really scared of them. The coolest thing about her is that she doesn't judge me for what I do or how I feel about guns and self-defense. She even went so far as to tell me that she would love to have me interview her sometime as to her feelings and tell her story. One of these days, I am going to have to take her up on that offer. She told me that even though she did not like what I did for work that she liked me as person and that was good enough reason to find common ground. This was probably the nicest thing an anti-gun person has ever said to me.

Let's face it, ladies; there are lots of people out there that hate guns. Heck, I have some family members who *really* hate guns and think that guns should all be banned so they don't get their "ass shot at by a bad guy". Yes, that is a direct quote to which I made a not-so-subtle recommendation to keep one's mouth shut in order to avoid being shot in the ass. As you can imagine, this was not well received. This does also tend to make family weddings a bit more interesting than usual. Case in point, the following conversation actually happened at a family wedding no so long ago.

Inflammatory family member as he is on the way out the door (I found out later that he deliberately sought me out just to pick a fight with me): "Hey feel free to 're-friend' me anytime." (on social media).

Me: "Um, not until you can keep your anti-gun opinions to yourself and respect my choices."

Inflammatory family member: Exit stage left, right when it started to get good.

But, don't worry, that wasn't the end of this conversation. Inflammatory family member's daughter decided to pick up where Daddy left off…

Daughter: "So, Jenny, what's new and what was all that about?"

Me: "Oh, things are good. You know how your dad always has to get into the middle of things. Especially if it is something he disagrees with."

Daughter: "Oh, right, don't you teach people about **guns** now?" (The word "guns" was heavily emphasized, like it was something evil and dirty and bad).

Me: "Yep, and guess who doesn't like it?"

Daughter: "Well, you should just ignore him, that's what I do."

Me: "I am doing my best, but it's kind of hard when he finds a way to get in my face about these things."

Daughter: "Well, do me a favor, just don't shoot my Dad!"

Me: Mouth agape, not believing what I just heard. My response went something like: "Um, really? I carry a gun on my hip every day and I haven't once shot anyone, intentionally or unintentionally, so I am pretty sure that you don't need to worry about that happening."

Inflammatory family member's daughter: "Oh. My. God. You carry a gun?! " Then she walked away...

This line of thinking is completely irrational. The thing that bugs me the most is that there is no middle ground on this or even an agreement to disagree. I respect the opinion and emotional response to not want to own guns. *But*, I do want the same courtesy from those people to respect my thoughts and feelings on the subject, along with my right and obligation to have the tools I need to defend myself and my family. My tool just happens to be a gun. I have also learned that we're not going to be able to rationalize this fear in people who refuse to be educated about guns or to see the other side of it. We've learned something in the last few years that I think most people in society fifty years ago knew very well: that not everyone likes you or thinks the same way you do. More and more every day, people are retreating into their own corners of the world and running to safety behind people who agree with them. It's increasingly rare to have to interact with people who actually, you know, disagree with you. So instead of "live and let live", society is turning into more of a "my way or the highway" kind of place. And the most popular way to deal with someone who disagrees with you intellectually is to dismiss them as crazy. That gives you complete autonomy to say all the crazy stuff *you* want to, because if you get called out, you can say the other person is just flat out nuts. In my opinion, the solution here is to focus on the positives, not dwell on those people who choose to fight with you. And as soon as that happens, you'd be surprised at how many new friends you'll make. So do what you can to ease the fears of the anti-gun friends and family members, and stick to what makes you comfortable. Don't let the few anti-gunners stop you from owning, using and enjoying guns just because they don't agree with you.

With that said, it's also all right to avoid the subject of guns altogether if you have friends and/or family members that just aren't interested in or are downright against guns. I do go out of my way to avoid the subject with these people at all costs if I can, but sometimes it's just not possible. Especially if they are just looking for a confrontation, like what usually happens with the inflammatory family member I just mentioned. It doesn't have to be a secret, but if you get the feeling that they would rather talk about how to solve a complex math problem or the cute thing that the kids did last night than guns, then leave it on the back burner. For example, we have friends with different backgrounds and beliefs, and some of those friends don't drink alcohol. Their decision does not affect us, but out of respect for them we just don't talk much about drinking. They know we drink on occasion, and yet they are still our friends. Crazy concept, I know.

I have another example for you: I have an acquaintance that has started to apologize for my gun-loving ways to people when they meet me for the first time. This usually happens right about the time that someone asks me what I do for work. My answer is that I am a firearms instructor. That is usually met with a raised eyebrow and a "how interesting". Come to think of it, maybe that "how interesting" response is more sarcastic than interested. I've learned to temper my enthusiasm around these friends. I never want to pressure people to be interested in or even talk about guns if they just aren't. There are plenty of other people that I can talk to about guns with excitement, that it's just not worth making others feel uncomfortable with it.

This acquaintance is the same person who introduced me to someone else as her "gun nut" friend one evening at a dinner. It really threw me for a loop because the gun stuff never really seemed to bother her before. Maybe she knew something more about the views people in our company than I did and wanted to make light of my profession before I had a chance to open my mouth. Either way, this was a hurtful experience. I would have rather had a sidebar conversation ahead of time to be given fair warning not to mention my profession at dinner, than have been treated like a *gun nut*. I immediately knew that from now on, guns, self-defense and my profession were off-limit topics between the two of us. I am not making apologies for what I do or what I think, but I don't need that kind of introduction to strangers either.

About a year later I found myself at yet another social gathering with this same individual and I am sad to report that I had gone from being a "gun nut" to being "crazy". I was sitting around having a conversation with a girl friend and I was explaining to her who the people around us were. When I mentioned the one acquaintance who would probably show up, I warned my friend that there would likely be an underhanded comment made if the acquaintance knew that the friend and I had similar interests and outlooks. Sure enough, the "how do you two know each other?" question was asked and upon replying that we had met while working on some town politics and discovered that we had several similar interests, the comment that I had warned my friend about came: "Oh, so you are crazy too!" People, I can't make this stuff up. It is really sad that in this day and age people are not allowed to have conflicting opinions without the other camp being "crazy". How about a little respect and common courtesy; is that too much to ask?

There is another dynamic at play here that I should address while we are on the subject. There is also the type of person out there that thinks it's cool that a woman is a) into guns, b) carries a gun and even c) teaches others about guns. This is best summed up another couple of quick stories.

I have a diverse network of friends. Some are friends by default, as they are friends of friends. Most of these people I really enjoy spending time with, others I put up with. Within this group is a person who thinks it is appropriate behavior to call attention to the fact that I might have a concealed weapon. This started happening shortly after this person found out what I do for a living. It started off as him asking me if I was "packing". The first time this happened it really caught me off guard and I kind of laughed it off and walked away. I really didn't think it was any of his business or anyone else's business if I had a gun on me. So I just swept it under the rug. However, that was the wrong way to handle this situation because it escalated from there. Sometime later this same person decided that it would be a good idea to pat me down when I walked into a room. I was so taken aback by this that I froze. I gave him a glaring look and told him to remove his hands from my body. He has not tried this again, and I don't think he will, but I did learn that the direct approach is definitely best when it comes to this stuff.

Another male acquaintance of mine (in fact he's Mr. to the Mrs. Acquaintance that I mentioned just a minute ago, the perfect couple!) also likes to make a big deal of my gun carrying. This also happens at inappropriate times. I was once introduced to some people as "My friend, Jenna, who is probably packin' heat right now". "She's an instructor and loves her guns; it's unusual for her to leave home without one". That was followed with the party I was meeting telling me "It's cool, my gun is actually in the car right now". Argh! I am happy that there are people out there who are comfortable with this idea of me carrying a gun, but can't there be a happy medium?

I guess what I am trying to say is that it's a good idea to get a feel for who is on board and who isn't and be mindful of those feelings when it comes to talking about that amazing new gun that you just got for Christmas. It's like talking about politics and religion; yes, I just went there. You need to tread lightly until you know that you are in the company of friendlies. Or, there is always the option of making new friends. The family thing can be a little more delicate. Just do the best you can, but you shouldn't have to sacrifice the things that are important to you in order to make others happy.

NORMAL, ABNORMAL AND DANGEROUS: THE NEW SITUATIONAL AWARENESS

I have really come to dislike the term "situational awareness". To me it has become an over-used buzz word that does not mean what people think it means. This is actually a military term that we have tried to adapt to be used by civilians, and I think it has lost something in translation. To begin with you don't have close air support or tanks backing you up, like the military does. I put it right up there with Cooper's Color Codes which is a set of alertness levels with escalating degrees of mental preparation for the use of force. Each level is assigned a color, hence the name. It is yet another military concept that we try so hard to adapt to civilian life. We must remember that our job as civilians is to get home safely to our families. Don't get me wrong, lots of people use Cooper's Color Codes and it works for them. It's just not how my brain works. While these things are descriptive of a situation in nature, they really don't give us an actionable plan to keep us safe.

So putting aside all the military and 'tacti-kool' connotations, what *is* situational awareness, really? To me it is being conscious of one's surroundings. Being aware of what is going on around you is an easy thing to do and it does not require hyper-vigilance, or even a great deal of time.

I have adopted a new model in order to be better able to put this into perspective, and more importantly into practice in my everyday life. This model is easy to understand and follow. I have even taught it to my son.

Here's the model: you need to know the difference between what is normal, abnormal and dangerous for a given environment. That's it.

I have spent countless hours discussing and dissecting this subject with my good friend and mentor, Marc MacYoung of No Nonsense Self-Defense[4]. Marc likes to say that it only takes two minutes a day to stay safe. Let me clarify: you don't need to walk around on high alert with your head on a swivel to have an idea of when things are about to go wrong.

You *do* have to know what is normal for your surroundings, however. Once you know what normal behavior for your surrounding looks like, you can see when something abnormal or dangerous is happening.

Normal is people going about their business, just trying to get through the day.

Abnormal is when people don't fit the mold of everyday behavior in that context.

Dangerous is abnormal behavior that can cause us injury or worse. When dangerous is happening we will need to rely on defensive behavior to stay safe.

It is rather easy to distinguish normal from abnormal, but distinguishing abnormal from dangerous is a whole different beast. Often, dangerous is disguised as pseudo-normal. So, our job is to pay attention and decide what is what as soon as we can.

Here is an illustration of what I am talking about. One night I was leaving a restaurant alone, at about 10:30 p.m. I was parked in an attached parking lot that was decently lit, but not overly bright. This parking lot does not make me feel safe when I am alone because it is in a downtown area and is attached to a motel parking lot where there are often a few people coming and going or standing outside for a smoke,

---

4   http://www.nononsenseselfdefense.com/

thus giving them a 'reason' to be hanging out in a parking lot at night. On this evening, the parking lot appeared to be empty. When I started towards my car I noticed that a pick-up truck that had been parked in the spot next to me began to back out and promptly blocked my car into its spot and stopped. At this point the driver of the truck opened his door, got out of the car and approached the back of my car. He was an older gentleman; he could have been my grandfather. The whole time I am watching this unfold I am thinking "what the heck"? "Did he just hit my car and now is checking for damage?" But that was not the case. At this point, since he did not hit my car and is not checking for damage, I have identified abnormal behavior. People usually don't stop their vehicles, block in the car next to them and get out of the truck.

Instead of retreating to a safe place or standing back and watching to see what was happening, I headed to my car. I honestly don't think that this is something I would do again in this type of situation. I think staying out of it and letting the offender leave is a better option than confrontation. By now I could clearly see that the man was taking cell phone photos of my license plate (again *abnormal*, but not yet *dangerous* behavior). This is about when I became acutely aware of where my firearm was and how I would get to it if I ended up needing it. The fact that he was taking photos of my license plate really got me going. At this time, I was about 10 feet away from the man so I asked him what he was doing. He immediately asked if it was my car. I told him it was and that I did not appreciate him taking photos of my license plate. The next thoughts to run through my mind were "Thank goodness that the car is registered in my husband's name *and* registered to my mailing address and not my home address!" The last thing I wanted was for this stranger to look up my name and address in some DMV database and know who I am if they didn't already, and where I lived. Scary! This behavior was indeed abnormal because people don't usually take photos of license plates in public. I have seen this happen on extremely rare occasions in my life, and it was usually due to a traffic incident or some similar issue. All I could think is that this man was taking a photo for some nefarious reason. Maybe he wanted to find out where I lived, for some reason, or to be able to track me down for something. This was also about the same time that we were fighting some polarizing political battles over gun rights in our small town and Jeff and I had been on the receiving end of threats of physical violence from the opposition. I had a fleeting thought that maybe some of those people were behind this photo shoot

He then told me that he had never seen a license plate like mine and that he always took photos of new plates he saw. This sounded like a bunch of BS to me, so I asked him to move his truck and let me pass. He seemed hurt that I was not happy to be having a conversation with him in a lonely, dark parking lot. I politely told him he was making me uncomfortable and I started to go back inside the restaurant. That is when he moved his truck. If he had not left at this time, I would have retreated to the restaurant because this is when I feel like things could have turned down the road to being a dangerous situation.

I am pretty sure that this man meant me no harm. If he had, I might have been in trouble because I was too stubborn to not listen to my gut and not engage with him. I think he was just a lonely old guy who thought I would be a nice person to have a conversation with.

I teach people how to recognize and hopefully avoid getting into violent encounters, and here I was engaging with a stranger in a parking lot late at night. All the way home I beat myself up for not following my own advice and not avoiding putting myself into harm's way to begin with. It makes no difference that I was armed that night; I still should have let him be when I saw him get out of his truck.

I should have watched this event unfold from inside the restaurant instead of giving in to my curiosity. While this situation was developing I was offended that this stranger had the nerve to violate my privacy in such a blatant way. The offended feelings and the fact that he was an old man, who did not appear to pose a physical threat to me, are what gave me the courage (for lack of a better word) to confront this individual. I am certain that I would have retreated to the restaurant right away if the man had tried to get closer to me than the boundary I had set when I walked to my car to confront him. I had many defensive options, such as telling him in a command voice that he was close enough, or to stop. I could have moved behind concealment and created more distance by getting behind another vehicle, or I could have drawn my weapon. The least confrontational option at this stage would have been to retreat to the restaurant. Looking back on this night, an important lesson was cemented for me: just because someone is committing offensive behavior doesn't mean you have to stand on principal and confront them. Let them go and deal with it later! If the abnormal had turned dangerous in this case, I might have been telling you a different story, or no story at all.

How do we know what is normal? It's quite simple, really. Every day you should notice things around you. That's it. Here are some examples; I'm sure you can think of others.

When you go for a walk in your neighborhood, what do you see? If it is daytime, I see people mowing their grass, washing their cars, or kids playing in the front yard. I see small groups of neighbors catching up on the sidewalk. I see people walking dogs, or riding bicycles. There are usually cars driving by (most of the time they are whizzing by me). So, when I happen to notice a car slowly creeping down the street, it will catch my attention because that is not normal behavior in this environment. This is when my radar tells me to look up and pay attention. If I see this happening I will keep an eye on the car and see where it goes. If it pulls into a driveway or stops in front of a house, I will take notice. Maybe it was as simple as the driver looking for a certain house that they had never been to before. If it stops near me I will really take note, because that is a red flag. I will likely stop and watch them with lots of interest and make sure they know I am watching them. In fact, this is usually about the time that Jeff will not-so-subtly grab his phone and take a photo of the license plate or tell me to make a note of it. In the event that this is something nefarious, you may be able to provide the information to the authorities someday and help them out. There isn't much reason for a car to need to approach me in my neighborhood. In this day and age of cell phones and hand-held communication devices they should be able to navigate without having to stop for directions.

The act of noticing abnormal behavior (or any type of behavior of others, really) has become somewhat of a lost art. I see so many people walking around with headphones on who are glued to their phones. It's the age of social media and email at our fingertips. Distractions are plenty, and they are not our friend.

There are certain normal things that we should all be able to recognize about our own neighborhoods. For example, in my neighborhood, if it is dark out, I don't see too many kids or people outside doing things. If there is a small group of older kids out, they are playing ball or something in a lit cul-de-sac. Neighbors may be chatting in a driveway. If people are doing other things other (activities that fall outside of the everyday normal), I will take notice, but go about my business.

Unfortunately most of the people I know are completely oblivious to their surroundings. This makes them a great target for crime. When I walk into a restaurant or a store I always take a look around to see who's in there and maybe notice if there is another exit. This doesn't have to be anything super obvious, just a passing glance to see who and what is around me. If I see something that raises a red flag then I might kick up my response a notch. But if everything looks the way it should I can go about my business. It's not all about being tactical – sometimes it's just about being an observant person. See, I didn't even have to be paranoid! If I am seated in a restaurant, without my husband, I always try and face the entrance so I can keep an eye on who is coming and going. If I am with Jeff then we usually bicker (my sister's word for it – Jeff and I like to think of it as an enthusiastic discussion) about who gets to watch the door. If we are lucky, one gets to watch the front door and the other gets to watch the back door; this way we have all our bases covered and there is no bickering necessary!

For me, another part of situational awareness is not intentionally putting myself into a vulnerable state. I mentioned that criminals try to attack people when they are distracted in the chapter on Carrying At Home. It works this way in public too. How many times have you seen a distracted mom, for example, leaving a grocery store? I see this just about every time I am there; heck, I have done this myself.

TIP: I can't help with the screaming kids or the diaper change, but I can offer some advice: always have your keys in your hand when you walk to the car! Not as a self-defense tool, but so that you are ready to go when you get there.

It looks something like this: a woman with an overloaded shopping cart and two screaming kids makes her way to the parking lot. When she gets to her car she starts digging through her oversized, overflowing purse or diaper bag to get to her keys so she can unlock the car, get the kids settled in and load the groceries. All of her attention is focused on immediate and up close 'problems.' While this is happening, does she ever look around to see who is near? My guess is not, because she is actively trying to do several things at once already. What if one of those kids needs a diaper change right at that moment? Now she's trying to change a diaper, juggle another kid or two, worry about the grocery cart rolling down the aisle and hitting another car and worry about who is going to be offended

As you leave the store, check your surroundings to see if anything seems out of the ordinary. Make a mental note of anyone who looks out of place, especially if they are watching you. When you get to your car, before you start to load kids or purchases, look around to see if anyone is approaching, then get the kids situated, lock the doors, and *then* worry about the groceries once everyone is in safely and you know what's happening around you. When you finish loading groceries look around again. Then get into the car. Just looking around three times – a total investment of six seconds – will go a long way to help keep you and your loved ones safe!

This practice works everywhere, not just at the grocery store. It is a great habit to get into *everywhere* you go. It works if you are alone or with a group. I suggest getting into this habit today!

This also has an unexpected side benefit, as you just might be surprised at the beauty you will see when you get into this habit. I don't know if it is because I am older now, or because I am more aware of the things around me but in the past several years I have seen so much beauty around me. An example of this is the Colorado sky. I don't know why this is, but they sky here is the most brilliant blue color. It is different to me than the sky in other places. It is spectacular. I don't think I would have ever seen the difference if I had not started paying attention to my surroundings. This is what I mean by "see the beauty around you". Once you open yourself up to notice things around you, you never know what will grab your attention. Sometimes it is something beautiful like the sky, or the landscape ahead of you, other times it may be that big rattling snake on the ground a foot away. Occasionally it might be something that is completely out of place and that you notice *before* it is too late to react or get out of there, or simply slow down and let it pass right on by you.

The fact is you already know this stuff. I am merely helping move this to the conscious part of your brain instead of having it buried under all the day-to-day stuff. Yes, there is danger out there, but you'll see more beauty this way.

Fringe Areas

The concept of "fringe areas" is also from Marc MacYoung and is a good follow-up to situational awareness. A fringe area is an area you travel through on your way to and from the crowd. It is usually a transitional area (like a parking lot), but can also be an area where immediate help is not an option. This could be because there are no people who can see or hear you if you were to cry out for help, like a public bathroom at a mall or a private room at a party.

The overwhelming majority of violent crime happens in fringe areas. That is why it is so important to understand what a fringe area is, and to pay attention when in one. The goal is to always have enough space and time to avoid a violent attack. Predators need prey, and not just any prey; they want prey that will give them what they want, and they want no risk of getting caught in the process. In rural Alaska, hundreds of miles from the nearest town, there aren't likely to be many two-legged predators – there isn't any prey! Likewise, there isn't a lot of violent crime *inside* a grocery store. Why not? Because there are cameras, employees and patrons who are all potential witnesses. A criminal doesn't want to get caught – that tends to put a damper on his ability to find a safe place to attack prey. So since we know that violent crime still happens, where does that leave for criminals to lurk? Fringe areas.

I've mentioned the most common fringe areas, parking lots and public rest rooms. Some other examples of fringe areas include:

- ☞ Alleys
- ☞ Stairwells
- ☞ Elevators
- ☞ Paths or underpasses
- ☞ Highway rest areas
- ☞ Remote area of a department store
- ☞ ATMs

The key element shared by these areas is isolation. Although we are seldom ever more than 100 yards from other people, walls, doors, vehicles and even what we're doing isolates us more often than we recognize.

We travel in and out of these areas daily. Being in one of these places is not dangerous by itself. A deserted parking lot is, after all, deserted. But you should notice when it is not deserted; who is there, and what are *they* doing in order to stay safe while in these areas? This is a great time to put away your phone or other distractions and pay attention!

Let's talk about parking lots for a moment. What is normal behavior for people in a parking lot? There's a lot of driving that goes on; how fast depends on whether they're coming in or going out. When I see people on foot in a parking lot they may be doing a number of things that I consider normal. They are either coming or going to a specific destination. They can be walking to or from their car or a store. They might be getting children into or out of the car, or loading up the car with things that they have just purchased. They could be having a conversation with friends before getting in the car to leave. There are also the people who are wandering around looking for their lost car; the distracted people on the cell phone, either talking or texting (they also tend to wander); the person sitting on a bench waiting for a ride; and the person smoking a cigarette. Let's also not forget about the woman looking for her husband who is now circling the parking lot in his truck, waiting for her to come out of the store. Been there, done that. These are not people that would worry me because this is all normal behavior in a parking lot. Something to watch for is people wandering or loitering in a parking lot. The examples above are normal behaviors for people in these areas. Remember, most people just want to get through their day. However, some types of wandering or loitering are *not* normal in parking lots. These are the ones you need to learn to notice, so that you can act appropriately.

Let's take a minute and expand on the group of people having a conversation in a parking lot for a minute because this is something that is rather common. The fact that the conversation is taking place in a fringe area does not automatically mean that these people have ill intent. Here are some normal behaviors that one may observe: the people in a group are facing each other and paying attention to one another; they may notice things happening around them, but they are not overly concerned with what goes on outside their conversation. If you walk by they keep on talking. If you walk by on the way to your car and the group suddenly changes its demeanor and the conversation stops, then *you* could be the reason that this happened, and you'll want to pay closer attention to the group. If, as you approach, the group starts to move away from one another and position themselves around you, then you have problems.

So how do we apply abnormal and dangerous behavior awareness to fringe areas? Abnormal behavior in a fringe area can be the guy who lost his keys and is wandering around looking for them. He means no harm and has a very specific task at hand, but he is not concerned with you being in the parking lot. Dangerous behavior in a fringe area is when you're about to come under attack. That translates into you being set up for an attack. Knowing when you can relax and zone out instead of paying attention to the things around you can mean the difference between possibly having to defend yourself or not. If you take a look around and see that everyone is participating in normal behavior for the place, then no worries.

Carry on with your day. If you see something that is abnormal, this is when you need to pay closer attention.

Another quote by Marc MacYoung that sums this up for me is when he often remarks: "the thing I love about deserted parking lots is that they are deserted." What he means is that there is no trouble to be found because there is no one there. You only need to be concerned about people's behavior when there are people around you.

An important thing to remember about fringe areas is that it is okay to retreat to safety instead of keeping on your current course. Often muggers will loiter around the entrances to follow people going into fringe areas. One example is loitering by the doorways at malls. To cover this loitering and waiting for prey, they often smoke. What is normal behavior for smokers when you pass them? They stay there and keep on smoking. If you were headed out of the mall to your car and you saw the smokers suddenly put out their cigarettes and begin to fan out around you, then you should go back inside where there are people. Then either wait for the smokers to move on or get a security guard to walk you to your car. There is no harm in being alert and asking for help. I'm also all for calling the cops. Every police officer I've ever talked to would rather have 1,000 false alarms that they responded to that ended up being nothing, than the one where you should have called but didn't. Just be ready to explain what you saw and why you thought it was trouble.

Here is another example of a fringe area and abnormal situations: I was in a large discount department store not long ago with my sister, when a woman came up to her friend who was standing near us. She told the friend that she just saw a man in the ladies room. She was visibly shaken. When I overheard this I told her that she needed to report this to the store management. She then saw the guy in the store and discovered that he actually was an employee of the store. My sister and I made her report this incident; if he was in there for any valid reason, such as to clean the rest room, he'd need to have announced his presence and waited to enter until the rest room was vacant. Nor had he put up 'closed' signs or other warnings such as those who have the legitimate business of cleaning or repairs do, to announce their presence. I actually told the woman that she needed to tell the management about this incident because a public restroom is a "classic fringe area." My sister and the two women who were talking to us all looked at me like I was nuts

No, I am not nuts, just aware! (See? There is the whole paranoid thing again!) Ladies (and gentlemen) *listen* to your intuition. A man in the ladies room is *not* normal. This type of thing should not be dismissed. It should be reported to the proper authorities.

Not long ago, I had my son with me at the mall. He was seven years old at the time, and very independent. He informed me that he needed to use the rest room and started walking down that long corridor. I caught up to him and told him that he would need to come into the ladies room with me instead. He was disappointed not to be given the freedom to use the rest room alone, but this turned into a good opportunity for me to explain why I did not want him using the public men's room at the mall, alone. One just never knows who may be lurking in there, and I am not in a position to go in ahead and make sure it's all-clear. I am pretty proud of giving my kid this level of awareness. He now reminds me to be careful and look for odd behavior whenever we are in a parking lot, parking garage, or headed to a public rest room. It's kind of a game for us. It doesn't have to be dark and scary. I like that we can see the fun side of it and have an open talk about what is normal behavior in these areas. It helps keep us all on the ball!

SETTING BOUNDARIES

Setting boundaries is very important when it comes to self-defense. The act of setting boundaries enables people to stay in their safety zone mentally and physically. If we do this right then we may avoid putting ourselves in a situation where we have to act in self-defense at all.

There is a perception in society today that when women set boundaries, they are being rude. In reality, when women set boundaries they are being assertive. However, there is a certain stigma attached to this behavior, especially when a woman does it; if it is done wrong it can come across as being bitchy or rude.

When I use the word "rude" in this context I am talking about the perception of being bad-mannered or pushy. Society can be a bit harsh when people don't react in a way that is expected. For example, if someone asks you if they can join you for a drink and you *politely* tell them that you are not interested, you might be considered rude. In reality, you were being honest as well as polite. Now, if you look them up and down and cast them off with a hand wave and an "Um, I don't think so", then you are being rude. See the difference?

Growing up we were taught to be polite to people, which is usually a good rule to live by. For this reason it is often extremely difficult for us to tell someone "no", or that we are not interested in an offer, or even to simply walk away if we feel uncomfortable. Please know that if your intuition tells you that something isn't right, then it is in your own best interest to listen to it. You have an obligation to yourself to do so. It is perfectly acceptable to follow your instincts at the risk of being perceived as rude.

Let me illustrate this point for you. Let's say you are out walking your dog when a car pulls up beside you, the window goes down and they ask you for directions (asking for directions is a great way to break the ice and it allows for a sense of normal even if it is only abnormal or dangerous in disguise). It is perfectly acceptable to politely tell the person seeking directions that you are sorry, but you are not able to help them and keep on walking. If they go on their way, it is possible they were actually looking for directions and they will go somewhere else for them. But, if they follow you instead, that is their way of changing the rules. It is no longer about getting directions, but it could be about *you.*

Another aspect of setting boundaries is that sometimes you have to be assertive for people to understand that you really mean it. I don't let strangers get into my personal space if I can possibly help it. Yes, this is harder in a crowd or even in a grocery store, but if someone wants to know what time it is, there is no reason that they need to get close enough to touch me to ask that question. If someone gets that close, I will give them a firm "That's close enough. Can I help you? " as I take a step back. This is a great time for them to ask you if you know what time it is. If they hesitate or if they take a step toward me at this point they are met with another, more emphatic "That's close enough! Can I help you?"

My reaction and statement reinforces the message I am conveying. You are close enough. Once I have established and they have respected my set boundary, I am willing to give them information. I am showing that I am willing to provide them with the help they need while maintaining my boundaries. In this example everyone wins.

The main reason that I don't let people get into my personal space in these situations is because information can be shared at a distance. Asking for or giving out directions at a distance, I am not in danger of immediate physical violence. If I should let people into my personal space and they then decide to use physical violence, then they are within range to do so. This is why people sometimes have the perception that "bad guys come out of nowhere". They have not come out of nowhere; they are just good enough at getting into range that we don't see them coming. Again, this speaks to knowing and recognizing what is normal and what is abnormal in a given situation, as discussed in a previous chapter.

For Ladies
(and the Men Who Teach Them)

Ladies, I encourage you to walk your own path on this journey of gun ownership and self-defense. I meet so many men who ask me what kind of gun they should get for their wife. My standard answer is none, unless she is the one picking it out. Choosing a gun, as I talked about earlier, is a very personal decision. Most times when men want to buy guns for their ladies they have this idea that the smaller the better. As we will learn, this is not always the best approach.

I have met a lot of women who have been gifted guns and they are always excited to take them out to the range and shoot them. The best case scenario is that they have a good outing and really enjoy shooting their guns. Far more common, however, is that the ladies find out that this "perfect" gun really isn't perfect for *them*. In these cases the person needs to approach the subject carefully, because if the gun was a gift, then admitting that it is not the best fit may upset both the gifter and the giftee. The other option is for the giftee to suck it up and learn how to shoot the gun anyway. Lots of times this happens and things are fine.

I am a bit of an example of this. I have already mentioned that I used to carry a Kahr PM9. I may not have mentioned that I really didn't enjoy shooting this gun. I bought it without shooting it first. I made the decision all on my own to buy this gun; there was no husbandly intervention or advice that went along with this purchase. My choice to purchase this gun was based solely on two criteria: it was chambered in 9mm and it was small/lightweight enough to comfortably carry on my person. My carry gun before this one ended up being much too heavy, which is where my motivation for smaller and lighter came from. I'll tell you, I got just what I wanted in a carry gun. I will also tell you the first time I shot it, I was not happy with much else about the gun. Nevertheless I decided to put in the time and effort and work of getting used to the gun. I am happy to report that I can in fact shoot the gun, and am accurate with it. That doesn't mean that I enjoy training with it, but I decided the trade-off was something I could live with, until I found a suitable replacement that I enjoyed shooting more.

As we are discussing ladies picking out a gun that is right for them, I should also mention that the best place for anyone to purchase a gun is on the shooting range. If we were able to shoot the different guns that we were interested in before we bought them, there would really be no guesswork left in the gun-buying process. This would also help in the process of narrowing down the field. If you are like me, then you may have several guns in the running to become your new tool.

And here's a newsflash, not all women are going to be able to comfortably shoot a tiny little pocket gun chambered in .380. Yes, these guns are small and easy to conceal but they are not easy or fun to learn on. These are tiny little guns, as I have already mentioned. The problem with this is that there is typically more 'felt' recoil with these small, lightweight guns. This is due to the fact that there is less mass to absorb the energy of the bullet, so there is more recoil for the shooter to feel than with the larger, heavier guns. The latter tend to be more pleasant to shoot because they absorb more of the energy of the bullet. The larger guns can be harder to carry though, so there are trade-offs. Gentlemen, what if instead of telling the woman in your life about the "most super-duper, perfect gun for her" you try saying something along the lines of "you might consider" such-and-such and "Here are some pros and cons about this gun or that gun". Then take her to a place where she can try out a variety of guns and choose the one that works for her. This is the fastest way to achieve hero status. I know this from experience.

To take this one step further, another thing the well-meaning men in your life sometimes do to derail your shooting education is interfere in your training. I this see time and time again and it drives me nutty. Men have this overwhelming need to protect their women; while this is certainly comforting, it can also be stifling. Gentlemen, please, don't go out and sign your wife, daughter, etc. up for shooting lessons or classes, and then interfere. Please, leave this to the professionals. (Wait, that's me!) Please, don't tell me that your wife *has* to have XYZ gun because it's the only one with a slide that she can rack. Racking a slide really doesn't have a whole lot to do with grip on the slide or the strength of your hands; it does have everything to do with technique. Please don't be that guy, let the lady learn this for herself! You just might be amazed at the things she will learn and the confidence she can gain if you let her experience this for herself. Hey, you never know, you just might learn something from *her* when it's all said and done.

I have a lot of husbands who want to come to class with their wives for whatever reason. In these cases, it is usually because they want to keep an eye on me or keep an eye on the wife. I have and will continue to politely invite the husband to register for the class with his wife, but I do not allow them to sit in the back of the class to observe. In doing so, I feel like I am giving the wife a chance to have her own learning experience without having to perform in front of a well-meaning loved one. We get this request for loved ones to observe classes a lot, both in the classroom and at the range. I also get the feeling that most of our female students are happy to be able to take a class without their husband or loved one watching them. I have also been told by a husband that his wife will have to unlearn the things that I will teach her at the range, if I teach her how to shoot on a normal size gun instead of the cute little .380 that *he* thinks she should shoot, because the recoil spring is light enough on the cute little .380 for her to rack the slide.

If these are the things that you are going to do for your loved one, then why, oh why, did you send her to me in the first place?!

Racking a slide is a hot button issue for me and probably lots of other instructors. I am sure that the military never had to teach all of the big burly men a good technique for racking a slide, because, well, you are big, burly men with nice big muscles and strong hands. I can pick on the military in this case, because I just so happen to be the daughter of a bad-ass former Airborne Ranger, who is a sharp shooter in every sense of the word (give the man *any* type of gun and he can hit the mark, at any distance) and am married to a former Air Force Officer, who shot competitively both in and out of the military. He is also a firearms instructor. When Jeff, my instructor/husband, was teaching me about racking the

TIP: If you are new to guns and have an overbearing person helping you through the process, it's perfectly all right to tell them to back off. Be polite and let them know that you appreciate their efforts, but also be firm and let them know that this is your journey and that you are prepared to come to your own conclusions. This approach might even earn you their respect!

slide, he got it all wrong *for me*, because he big and strong (and handsome, oops, sorry we are off topic). My point is that until you well-meaning men have struggled with how to rack a slide when you are of inferior strength and have not yet developed a solid technique (as the teacher has) you really can't know what others can or can't do.

I also get weary of women telling me that their *last* instructor or loved one didn't tell or teach them to do something *that* way. Maybe that just means that she is trying to reconcile this new information based on a previous experience. Actually, I am a big fan of that; I don't want to minimize any of the training that people may already have taken before they come to me. However, I also want to help people, especially women, find efficient ways to do things that previous instructors may not have taught them.

There are certain issues that many women may face when it comes to the shooting sports that men may not have to overcome, and therefore would not be aware of. This does not mean that men can't teach women; however, I believe that it takes a really good understanding of these issues to properly teach women how to deal with them. For the guys out there who are around a lot of female shooters, and have some experience with the issues they face, you may be ahead of the curve!

Purse carry is a great example of this. If a man does not actually carry a purse or bag and has not been taught about purse carry from a qualified female, he should not pass information about this topic onto the ladies. This should be a no-brainer. Now, if said man actually carries a purse and practices with it on a regular basis, then he may be qualified to be giving out advice on this matter. This also goes for men who write reviews on products that they don't actually use. Think purses, bra holsters and the like. If you don't have any experience with a product or situation, how can you effectively teach about it?

> **TIP:** I was once in an instructor's class and witnessed a male colleague try on a bra and "flashbang" holster to learn how to teach women to properly use one. This man can and should be teaching women!

When it comes to "potty training" (Kathy Jackson's term), ladies, heed this warning. If a man tells you to remove your gun and place it in your underpants while you use the restroom, you have two options: option one is to run. Run far away, because the guy has not taken the time to do the proper research into this issue and how it works for women. Your second option is to nod, smile and disregard. You can confidently employ option two, because I am about to tell you how it really works.

You are on the range and need to use the restroom. This means that you are well hydrated, so good for you! The first thing to remember is that you should **never** remove your gun from its holster at any time during this process! Now that you have made the promise to leave your gun in the holster I will give you the steps to a worry-free potty break at the range, or anywhere else you may have to use a rest room with a gun on your belt.

Put the lid down. We do this so nothing has the chance to fall in. I don't know about you, but I might be tempted to go in after my 1911 so I take this step very seriously.

Un-fasten your belt and pants and pull them down while you secure the holstered firearm with your hand (so it does not tip over, as you lower your pants, this is one more reason to make sure your holster passes the tip test before using it).

Fasten your belt around your knees so it is taut and your holster is secure with your gun safely inside of it.

Raise the lid, and do your business.

When you are done, close the lid again.

With a firm grasp on the holstered firearm raise your pants back to your waist and secure your belt.

Get back to the firing line ASAP!

If you need to use the restroom in public while carrying concealed, then this process is the one to follow. It is good practice to try and get the stall closest to the wall (on your gun side) while using a large public rest room with stalls. This will help keep your carry status secret from the prying eyes of curious little children who like to look under the stalls. Having them scream "Mommy, that lady has a gun" might not be in your best interest.

Carrying your gun in a location other than on your belt probably does not pose these issues, so just leave the gun safely where it is and don't fiddle with it, and you'll be just fine.

Speaking of range protocol for the ladies; have you ever tried to reholster your sidearm at the range, only to find that you can't see your holster because part of your anatomy is in the way! Ladies, I am talking about your chest here. Please know that, yes we want you looking as you put your gun into your holster, and it is perfectly acceptable to reach over with your non-shooting hand and move body parts out of the way in order to be able to see your holster. Just make sure that you are not putting your non-shooting hand in front of the muzzle of the gun when you do this. This is best done by reaching to the outside edge of your chest and smushing parts (breasts, for example) into your body so that they become lower profile for a moment, and you are able to now see your hip. I know this explanation makes more sense when you see rather than read it; it really needs a demonstration. Use your imagination, though – you'll get the idea.

Another thing I see a lot in this business is people coming to us (usually women) and telling us that they are not allowed to shoot/carry a gun etc., in any way other than how they were taught by so-and-so (usually a well-meaning man in their life). Now, I don't want to keep bashing men, but in my experience they are the biggest culprits when it comes to these things. Not *all* men do this and some that do, don't even know that they are doing this, so that leaves us with a very small sample size of actual bozos. The other two categories we can work with! My favorite example of this is when we are teaching speed reloads on the range and a woman refuses to drop her magazines on the ground. I see this all the time. It is usually because their well-meaning men have told them that they can never drop a magazine on the ground. To that end, I always teach the ladies how to take apart and clean the magazines when they get home. We teach self-defense applications and it is more effective to get rid of the magazine when you are done with it than it is to try and hold onto it (unless of course, you are performing a tactical reload, but that is not the instance that I am referring to in this case).

LEGAL ISSUES AND USE OF FORCE

I need to remind you that I am not an attorney and I have no designs on becoming one. Therefore, I am not allowed to hand out legal advice. However, I feel strongly about knowing what the laws are regarding the ownership and use of firearms, concealed or otherwise, where you live. I have immersed myself in the study of the use of (and aftermath of using) deadly force. I also make a point to offer classes on this (taught by a qualified attorney) because it is so important. There is a huge difference between the "law" and the "legal system". Both are important and I will attempt to touch on each one. Understanding the difference between the law and the legal system will really help you navigate this territory.

Think of the law as the set of rules by which upstanding citizens live their lives. We have laws that we abide by every day. Some we like and some we don't. It's basically the rules of the road for society. Without laws it would be hard to know what is expected of us in society.

The law may tell you that it is acceptable to act in defense of yourself or of your property (in certain states), but knowing the unintended consequences and the repercussions of acting in self-defense will go a long way to help you be more prepared for the legal aftermath of using deadly force. For one thing, raising "self-defense" in court is a whole other beast. You need to have a good understanding of what this means for you.

You will need an attorney who understands how to defend this claim, and you will need an amazing support system to help you through the dark days of what will likely follow. The emotional, physical and financial stress of a deadly force encounter can change your life overnight. Knowing what to expect and how to work through this is the key to success.

The legal system is the part of the equation that you may have to endure even if you did everything "right" in acting in self-defense. This is the part where you will deal with the police, attorneys, courts etc. The legal system can be a beast, and since "self-defense" has become a buzzword, you will really need to have acted properly and know how to articulate to the right people why you took the steps you did at the time the event occurred. I know this is a lot to take in. The bottom line is that if you did everything right, and know (and can articulate!) why you acted the way you did, it may still not be enough. The good news is that there are resources out there to help you navigate these waters. I will provide some more information on these resources in this chapter.

You need to educate yourself on this subject of self-defense law and the legal system, and, no, your crazy uncle, or your neighbor's husband, or worse, "the guy on the internet" is not the type of expert I am talking about (to quote Jeff Meek). If you have any questions about what the law actually says, then you need to read it and interpret it for yourself, or even speak to a lawyer to get a clear understanding. There are lots of great resources out there that can help with the interpretation, but these resources are not the law! *You* and *you* alone are responsible for knowing the law and abiding by it.

I would also be remiss if I did not ask you to think about the question "Why do we shoot in self-defense?" Is it to kill, maim, or wound?   No! These are terrible reasons to shoot someone in the name of self-defense. The one and only reason we should ever pull the trigger in self-defense is to **stop a threat** from killing or seriously injuring ourselves or another person.. Once the threat has been neutralized, then we stop shooting.

There are so many cases in the news of self-defense shootings where people get convicted of murder in the first degree because they have continued shooting once the threat has been neutralized. Marc MacYoung says that one of the hardest things to do in human nature is to stop aggression once you have started it. He says that we are not wired to do that. Intensive training is the only way I know of to prepare us for those force decisions without actually engaging in violence. I really can't stress enough that your mindset needs to be in the frame of *stop the threat*. Remember that we have to justify using deadly force for *each* and *every* time we pull the trigger, not just the first time.

Here is a specific example of this type of situation: The Oklahoma City pharmacist, Jerome Ersland. In the case of Mr. Ersland, he was working in his pharmacy one evening when two men came in in an attempt to rob the place. It has been suggested that the robbers had cased the place and knew when narcotics and cash would be accessible. It was these items that they were after in the robbery. The robbers entered the store and ordered employees to hand over the drugs and the money. The robbers fired shots, one of which grazed Ersland's hand, according to one report I found on the case. Ersland pulled a semi-automatic pistol from the pocket of his pants, fired, and the bullet struck one of the robbers in the head. The robber fell to the floor and lay there unconscious as Ersland chased the 2nd robber from the store. When Ersland returned to the store, he retrieved a second gun from a nearby drawer and proceeded to fire five more shots into the chest of the unconscious robber. According to the medical examiner, these proved to be the fatal shots. Ersland was convicted of first degree murder, as the second round of shots were characterized as a separate event from the first shot that incapacitated the robber. My impression of this event, and the jury agrees, is that Mr. Ersland went into the encounter with a mindset of "I need to shoot to kill... and keep shooting until he's dead."

That is the difference between "shoot to kill" and "shoot to stop the threat."

As seen in this example, if you think of "shooting to stop a threat" instead of "shooting to kill" you may just set yourself up to be in a better frame of mind if you are ever in a position to defend your life with deadly force. It's about survival, not vengeance. In too many cases the victims of the violent crimes have it in their heads that they need to shoot to kill their attacker, and so they wind up getting convicted in what would otherwise have been a justified shooting in self-defense.

When people say that we should shoot to kill, I think that they are referring not to the action of shooting itself, but where we should aim – but that's a different thing altogether. I agree with the idea of what to aim at as being vitally important. We should always *aim to stop a threat* instead of firing a warning shot (a whole separate issue, as well as a terrible idea) or taking the time to place a perfectly aimed shot in someone's kneecap. Remember, we are only shooting to neutralize a threat and we need to do that as quickly and efficiently as possible. Under adrenal stress, I would like to have the biggest possible target, and one most likely (if hit) of stopping the threat in time enough to allow me to get home safely to my family.

We always hear people tell us that we should aim for center of mass on a human being. While this may be a reliable place and a large target to aim at in most circumstances, I do not recommend this as your primary target. I believe from all of the training that I have had that the best place to aim at to stop a threat is the cardiovascular triangle area on a human target. This is roughly from the armpits to the Adam's apple on a person. The reason for this primary aim point is because this is where a person's vital organs are located, and a hit there is the best chance of humanely stopping them from furthering their attack on you. When I say humanely I mean that it is much more likely that one shot will be able to thwart an attack than several poorly placed shots.

Instead of thinking in terms of aiming at center mass it may help to think in terms of aiming at center chest. The center of the chest gets you much closer to hitting the parts of the human body most likely to result in quickly stopping the threat.

Our second aim point should be the pelvis or pelvic girdle. This is a highly effective target. There are major arteries here and a person will not be physically able to advance on you if this area has been shattered. Besides that, if you ever need to point a gun on that region of a male attacker, he will likely think twice before continuing to attack you, out of sheer terror of having a weapon pointed at this region. (Why, oh why, does this make me chuckle?)

Our third aim point is the head. Think of this as a last resort in the target selection process as it's a relatively small target and is extremely mobile. It's hard enough to shoot a stable target in a high stress situation, but introduce a moving target and it becomes exponentially more difficult. If the head is all you can see, then this gets bumped up the list, but if you have other options available, go for those first. The head usually ends in the highest percentage of "stopping shots" but, as mentioned, it is the hardest target to hit unless you can get close enough to your threat (point-blank range) to make this more effective shot. One example of this was the man who took a little girl hostage in a store a couple of years back. An off-duty police officer was able to get into point blank range and end the armed standoff very effectively with one shot to the head. The little girl was able to go home to her family that day.

The definition of "self-defense" from the Merriam-Webster dictionary is as follows: "*The act of defending yourself, your property, etc.; skills that make you capable of protecting yourself during an attack*".[5] I disagree with the part of defending your property with *deadly physical force*. And this is why: there is no amount of property, no matter how cool or cutting edge or expensive it may be, that is more valuable than a human life. So no matter how much you love your car, for example, it's just a car and it can be replaced. A human life can never be replaced.

---

5   http://www.merriam-webster.com/dictionary/self-defense

You can, however, defend your property with an appropriate amount of physical force. This is any force used on another person. If you remember, I talked about the time a guy came to my door under the guise of wanting to service my satellite dish. In that instance, I used physical force on him when I shut the door in his face. This is a perfect example of using the amount of force necessary to stay safe.

We hear stories in the news all the time where people are shot while committing burglary or while fleeing the scene of a crime. In many of these cases, I just cringe when I hear what the circumstances were. The one case that immediately comes to mind was when a man left the safety of his home, where he was not in immediate danger, to shoot at an individual who was attempting to break into his car. If only he had remembered (or better yet, had trained with the mindset) that "Good people carry firearms to defend innocent life, not to fight over personal property or to protect their own egos." to quote Kathy Jackson in "The Cornered Cat: A Woman's Guide to Concealed Carry"[6]. It could have saved someone from being shot in the first place. I can't remember now, or if it was ever mentioned in the news, whether the bad guy lived or died but that is beside the point. Calling the police and hunkering down would have been the right thing to do under those circumstances.

In some states you are legally allowed to use deadly force in defense of property in a few situations. If you live in one of these states I recommend thinking over the moral impact of doing so *before* you are actually faced with the situation.

One other thought while we are on the topic of defense of property. There is a huge difference between 'legally allowed to' and 'morally should'. Please remember when it comes to this stuff that as sad as it is, your pets are actually property. I love my dogs (even my black lab Vader, who eats a dozen socks or dozens of LEGOs in one sitting, all to have an upset stomach an hour later), but that doesn't mean I should shoot a person in defense them (if it were legal to do so in my state, that is),

---

6   The Cornered Cat: A Woman's Guide to Concealed Carry.
Kathy Jackson: White Feather Press, LLC, 2010

nor would I be able to justify this to myself morally. This also goes for horses, cats, fish, alligators (yes, I have a friend who has an alligator) and any other type of pet you may have. How do I know when it is appropriate to use deadly force? This is a question that it is to know the answer to. If I am going to teach people how to shoot and/or how to carry a gun for the purpose of defending their lives, I also need to tell them *when* it is time to use that level of force. There are different laws on this in all 50 states. I urge you to read the laws that apply to you and where you live, and ask an expert to fill in any blanks for you. Attorneys, police officers, and other professionals in the application of the law are the experts I am referring to.

This one gets a little tricky because as you may recall, I am not an attorney. I can't give you legal advice. I can, however, give you some resources about where to find the answers. Most of what I am about to discuss here comes from Massad Ayoob[7]. He has written numerous books on this subject including "In the Gravest Extreme" and more recently "Deadly Force: Understanding Your Right to Self-Defense", a follow-up to the first book. These are must-read for all gun owners. I can also highly recommend Massad Ayoob's MAG40 class, which goes into great detail on the topic.

The Armed Citizens' Legal Defense Network[8] (ACLDN) is another amazing resource for gun owners who are interested in self-defense law. I am an affiliate instructor for ACLDN and cannot recommend them enough. ACLDN is just what it says in the title, it is a network of professionals from the self-defense industry, who can help with your legal defense (expert witnesses and monetary help) if you ever get into a self-defense incident. Another value of The Network is the educational materials that they send you when you join. At this time, there are eight full length lectures on DVD to help you learn about what actions are justifiable, what to expect and how to deal with the legal aftermath of a defensive incident.

---

7   http://massadayoobgroup.com/
8   http:// https://www.armedcitizensnetwork.org/

Figure 31: Vader is guarding ACLDN
booklets. He is always happy to help! Photo
by Jenna Meek.

According to Massad Ayoob, deadly force is legally justified when there is an *"Immediate and otherwise unavoidable danger of death or grave bodily harm to the innocent"*. All of these criteria have to be met. If you can avoid using deadly force by running to safety and getting out of the situation, then by all means, that should be plan A.

'Castle Doctrine' (the right to self-defense in your home) and 'Stand Your Ground' (removal of the duty to retreat before engaging in self-defense) laws have been all over the news in the last couple of years. These terms are also being misused on a regular basis. You should know what the laws where you live actually say and be able to explain these laws and why they apply to you, if you are ever in a situation where they do, in fact, apply to you.

In my state, we have a 'Castle Doctrine' type of law. It basically says that you are authorized to use deadly force against an intruder if a certain set of criteria have been met. If the criteria have been met and you fall under this law, you will be immune from criminal and civil prosecution. The intent of such a law is that you don't have a duty to retreat anymore.

Your home is considered your last place of retreat, as opposed to when you are out and about. If you are out in public and can retreat, do it!

In my state the laws for use of force and deadly force are different inside and outside of the home. If this is true of the state you live in, I highly recommend learning those differences! The laws regarding use of force in my state say that force has to be met on a level playing field, so to speak. Unless you are in danger of being killed or receiving grave bodily injury, you are not authorized to use deadly force in my state. Again, you have to know what the rules are.

You should know what the rules are in the places you travel to with your gun, for that matter. This goes for more than just using deadly force. These laws change from state to state and if you are traveling to a state that you have reciprocity in (allows you to carry your firearm with the permit issued in your state or another state), you are now held to the laws and standards in that state and you'd better be well-versed in what those laws and standards are.

I spend a lot of time in Texas and I did more traveling than usual last year, so I am especially interested in knowing what places I can and can't carry in, and how to deal with the police if I am ever involved in a traffic stop while armed. Some states require you to immediately disclose your status to the officer pulling you over, and some don't. Knowing the difference can make a huge impact on how well the rest of your day goes. Also, there are many states that have a 51% law (you are not permitted to carry a weapon onto the premises of any establishment that earns 51% or more of its revenue from the sale of alcohol) when it comes to carrying into a premise that sells alcohol for on- or off-site consumption. Think restaurant with a bar; even if you are not drinking, is carry in these places permitted? There is no such law where I live, but this does exist in many of the states that I travel to. So I am responsible for knowing whether the law applies in that place or not. I recommend printing out the laws for the various places that you plan to visit and keeping them nearby so you that can refer to them whenever a question arises. Handgunlaw.us[9] is a great resource for this information.

There is another topic that I need to touch on while we are discussing legal aspects of firearms and carry, and that is the crime of 'brandishing' or 'menacing' (depending on where you live). In Colorado, since it is legal in most areas of the state to open carry a weapon, we do not have a law against brandishing. Brandishing is the act of showing your weapon. We do, however, have a law against menacing. 'Menacing' requires intent to scare or harm someone. I encourage you to put in the time and do the research with regards to what applies where you live.

I often hear people say that you should never pull out your gun unless you are going to use it, because the act of pulling your gun is a crime". Well, yes – in most cases that is true. But let me ask you a question; if you are being attacked and pull out your gun, and the bad guy sees the gun, abandons his attack, and starts running away – do you have to shoot him in the back as he runs away, just because you pulled out your gun? No! Of course not! That would not be good. So the short answer is that you should only pull out your gun if you intend to use it, but if the act of getting your gun out deters the attack and you don't have to use it, then you are better off. It is easy to explain to law enforcement at that point why you are standing there with a gun.

This brings me to my next point. There are two things you should always have with you in the event that you choose to carry a gun. Those two things are a cell phone and your Concealed Handgun Permit (or whatever it is called in your state). The reason for this is simple. First, and most importantly, you must win the race to call 911, as the first person to go on record gets logged in as the victim; right or wrong, this is the way it goes. Second, if you EVER have to pull your gun, you need to be able to prove to the responding officer that you are the good guy and that you are permitted to be carrying a

9   http://www.handgunlaw.us/

weapon in the first place. Once that is established, you can put the other information you have learned about the legal aspects of carrying, pulling and/or using your weapon to good use.

Training!
How to Achieve Your Goals

Now that you are on your way to responsible, safe gun ownership you should really consider getting some training. In many states, some kind of training is required in order to obtain a concealed carry permit. In my opinion, the required amount of training is not enough. In many cases it takes much more than the required minimum amount of training before one is fully prepared for the responsibility of carrying a gun for self-protection.

In many states people who are seeking concealed carry permits are required to take a class as part of the permit application process. In some cases, there are really no requirements for what that class has to include, other than that the instructor has to have some sort of credentials to teach. In many cases, this means having an NRA Instructor Certification. Live-fire training may or may not be required, depending on the state. No matter what the training requirements may be in your state to obtain a permit, it is a little scary to me that after one class people may be considered "good to go"!

What Jeff and I tell our students is this: taking an introductory course in gun safety and operation is a great place to *start*. Most of the time people are looking to get a permit, take the required class and call it a day with their training. This is no problem if you never find yourself in a situation. Where this can be an issue is if you should ever find yourself in a situation where you ever need to *use* that concealed weapon.

There is *so much* more that needs to be learned.

For instance, do you know how to use the gun as a self-defense tool? When should you use it on an attacker? More importantly, when not to? How will you get it out of the holster? How long does it take you to get the gun from its holster and how close does an assailant have to be before you are justified in doing so? If you show an assailant your gun, do you then have to shoot them, even if they abandon their attack on you? Can you legally shoot someone in the back as they are running from you? What if they are running away from you but toward your children? Is it still not justified?

What are the laws in your state pertaining to the possession and use of guns? Are you allowed to have a loaded gun in the car? What will the legal aftermath of a defensive shooting be like, and how will you deal with it? What should you tell the responding officers? What should you tell the 9-1-1 operator? What do you tell your friends and family afterwards?

Most of these things cannot be crammed into the state's minimum required amount of training to obtain a permit, nor should it be. Most instructors aren't even remotely qualified to be teaching this stuff, even if they do have a fancy piece of paper with their name on it. These topics need to be taught – and discussed and seriously thought about by you, the gun-owner – in order to provide the necessary knowledge for responsible gun-ownership.

Responsible gun ownership. Those are some very big words. Those issues I listed are often overlooked — or worse assumed to know already — by many people who own firearms. In doing so they give rise to the fears about guns that many people have. Don't be the kind of gun owner your friends are concerned to be around or let their children be around.

The next point is how to find the best firearms instructor for *you*. This is a loaded question (pun only slightly intended).

It is really hard to choose an instructor based on their own description on a web page. I know, I have been there!

The best way to interview a firearms instructor is to get in touch with them and find out how they are going to help you reach *your* goals when it comes to learning about guns. Reaching your goals is what it is all about. Any good instructor should be open to chatting on the phone or via email in order to provide you with information to help you make your choice. If you need suggestions on some questions to ask of potential instructors here are a few. Ask them "What was the last firearms class *you* took?" "Can I talk to one of your former students?" "Are you insured?" "Have you or your company ever had to interact with law enforcement?" "Have any other professionals vetted your class?" "Can I talk to them?", as well as any other questions you can think of. Knowing the answers to these questions can go a long way towards helping you choose an instructor who is reputable.

One of the first things you should also do is decide what type of training you are looking for. Do you want to become a competition shooter, or learn how to use a gun as a self-defense tool? Maybe you want to learn military tactics and learn how to clear houses of zombies. Or maybe you just want to learn how to be safe and effective with your weapon of choice so that you can shoot as a hobby.

This is a very personal and individual thing; there is no right or wrong answer here. Different schools will have different specialties – ours happens to be civilian self-defense using a firearm. The most important thing is that your instructor has the proper qualifications, mindset and background to teach you what it is that you are looking to learn, and not what they *think* you should learn. This should be evident if you start asking questions. If a firearms training institute is honest with you and with themselves, they'll absolutely tell you what they can do, but more importantly, what they can't (or won't) do. If someone tells you otherwise, I'd keep shopping. There is no better way to pick an instructor than talking to former students.

I've read a lot of interesting – and some complete hogwash – stuff on the websites of some of these places. You can easily avoid the hogwash if you speak to a few students or others who've had experience with the training institute. A huge bonus is getting first-hand referrals from other instructors. It's one thing if some random person says this place is great, but if another instructor can vouch for them, that's about as good an indicator as there is. Most instructors will not throw out a recommendation unless it's the real deal – after all, their reputation is on the line as well!

Feel free to ask for a resume to see where instructors have been and who they have learned from. Most instructors are proud to tell you how they got to where they are. If they aren't, then that could be a red flag. Keep on reading to find out more about mindset and background and why they are important to *your* training goals

I believe (as do many of my colleagues) that there are a number of "pillars" or "backgrounds" that people can have when it comes to guns and what qualifies people to teach others. There are five pillars that I would like discuss. Please know that each of these backgrounds is important and valid. Please also know that having background in one or all of these does not necessarily give one all the tools that they need to teach others about guns or how guns apply to the goals that *you* might have. I am in no way discrediting *any* of these backgrounds; I just want people to understand the vast differences in the mindsets these backgrounds have on our outlook and firearms training. I am especially interested in how these mindsets translate to the world of self-defense, as that is what I teach.

The five pillars that I want to discuss are listed below, in no particular order:

- Military
- Law Enforcement
- Competition
- Hunting
- Civilian Self-Defense

Let's start with #1, the military. The goal of the dedicated men and women in the military is to accomplish the mission as laid out for them. The secondary goal is to do everything possible to get their teammates and themselves home safely. This is what the brave men and women of the military are taught how to do. I might also add, they know how to fight and stay alive (because they train constantly for it, this is their *job*) and that they are *good* at it. They use the best tools available to them: military grade weaponry, tactical clothing, boots, night vision, and body armor, to name a few. They also work in teams designed to best accomplish the mission at hand. They have Intel on the ground and air support at the ready. They are not exactly "going it alone" out there. They can rely on this equipment to be there when they need it most and to help give them every advantage they need to have while fighting the enemy. This includes tanks, artillery and planes to make buildings go away. They have this equipment because they know what kinds of things they will encounter in the field. They also have Military Rules of Engagement (ROE). The rules for the military are completely different than our civilian ROE. The ROE for the military have nothing to do with common law or the legal system in this country. However, we as civilians are held to that lofty standard and must be experts on the law. Don't assume that because people have a military background that they are experts on the law, the tactics or the tools of the armed civilian

The second pillar, Law Enforcement, is a different kind of beast altogether. The mission of policemen and women is simple; they have to stop/catch bad guys. Wow, not a job that I would want, especially given those big heavy duty belts they have to wear on patrol, you know, the gun, flashlight, hand cuffs, etc.. I have the utmost respect for ALL law enforcement. You see, the police have a "duty to act" (we'll talk about how this relates to self-defense a little later). It is the job of the police to stop and capture criminals. They also have the burden of investigation of crimes, and lots and lots of paperwork. They are trained accordingly to maintain and upgrade these skill set. They have to qualify on the shooting range every so often, and keep their skills sharp.

But, did you know that the most important tool a cop has with him is not his gun?   It's his radio! With the push of a button back-up will be on the way for support. Did you also know that cops are supposed to wait for back-up before entering a dangerous situation? Their #1 priority is their own safety, *not* dying to save an individual. (This is the way it should be, by the way) Once their safety has been secured, then they can proceed with the task at hand, whatever that may be.

Also know that laws apply to the police much differently than they do for civilians. The cops have a *duty to act*, because they're sworn officers specifically to fulfill this duty. That means if they see a crime happening they are legally obligated to do something. *You are not.* Also they're afforded a lot more leeway in performing that duty than you and I are – and that's not a bad thing, it just is. It is also usually assumed that the police are experts on how the law applies to us as civilians, but that is not always the case.

I would be remiss if I did not bring up a point that Jeff made to me when in discussion of this piece, which is that, "*Some* of the guns skills from these first two disciplines translate to us in a self-defense situation. Some don't. Military and Law Enforcement for example, are often times headed *into* the danger – hopefully, we aren't. Also I personally don't really care if the guy runs away. Military/Law Enforcement very much cares about that." (Thanks, Dear!)

In #3, Competition, we see another aspect of firearms ownership come forward. The competitive shooter is a person who has fantastic gun handling skills and accuracy. This is their whole goal; to be fast *and* good, at the same time. The emphasis here is on "fast." Every serious competition shooter will tell you that accuracy is good and all but if you aren't fast, you won't win. That speed doesn't always translate well for us. Sometimes the only speed that matters for us is how fast we can run! Or how fast we can dial 9-1-1, or how fast we can get to our car and get away. By "good", I mean accurate in hitting where and what you aim at. It's easy to be one or the other, but being both accurate and fast at the same time is quite a challenge. I know this from experience.

The competitive shooters have it all. Competitive shooting is a thing of beauty and watching these shooters is inspirational! The thing that is easy to overlook when it comes to certain types of competition is that it is not exactly "real world," even if it's billed as "practical shooting." What I mean by this is that the tools that competitive shooters use are very job-specific. They have "race" guns, holsters, ammo and the list goes on. There are rules in competition that makes it run smoothly and be more interesting to watch, but it doesn't reflect the "real-life" situations you might find yourself in, in a gun fight on the street. For instance one "branch" of competition always has you start the course of fire while standing in a "starting box".

It's also worth noting that competition guns tend to be larger – maybe much larger, and heavier than day-to-day carry guns. Many now even have cool reflex sights and lightened triggers and all sorts of fun stuff. The holsters also tend to be specially geared for speed of the draw. (These are not always, if ever, safe for every day carry on the street.) There is even historical and horseback shooting competitions where participants dress up as cowboys. Competition shooting can be fun.

There are also some other interesting skills that can be misleading – in every competition that I'm aware of, the competitors can walk through the stage and scope it out before they shoot it. They already know who the bad guys are, where the hostages are, where the walls are, everything. We don't usually have that luxury when it comes to self-defense. So let me make one thing clear: I'm a fan of competition, but *only* if it's taken for what it is – competition. Just like everything else, don't assume it's more than it is.

Now, that's not to say that some of the skills used in competition won't transfer over to the self-defense world, because they would. You need to know the best way to pull a trigger and how to effectively manipulate your gun, and those are skills that become second nature the more you practice them. I do think that there is value in competition, just as there is value in the other pillars, but the rules are different from civilian self-defense. The mindset is different and the tools are different. Treat competition for what it is, a friendly, fun, comparison of skill sets. We run into problems with this when we make the assumption that these skills transfer perfectly to the other four pillars, which they don't. But, if we take this for what it is and not more, we will be just fine.

Now we come to the fourth pillar, Hunters. The goal and mindset of the hunter started out as a means of survival. These days, it has also become about sport, as the need for an individual to kill animals to eat isn't always a necessity. We have slaughterhouses, markets, and professionals who do it for us. But, let's look at it from the standpoint of survival and not sport. In a survival mindset if you didn't kill, you didn't eat. I can think of no better motivation to be a hunter. Hunters *had* to be good at their craft in order to feed their families. When I speak of hunting as a "craft" I'm thinking of all the things that go into being a successful hunter; for example, most times you have to get up early in the morning to get into position for observing the animals, or in order to lay in wait until it is time to strike; you can't let the prey know that you are there; you have to be patient (I guess that leaves the hunting to Jeff!); and of course you require the knowledge and training to use hunting firearms effectively and safely.

So hunters have worked at this craft and presumably learned the best practices through trial and error, and over time the techniques have become solid and have been handed down through the generations. Without the skills of our ancestors, where would we be?

One should note, of course, the different equipment that applies to hunting vs. self-defense. For hunting, rifles and shotguns are the primary weapons most of the time and for self-defense we usually (not always) have pistols. If you are trained with one but need to use the other, it can be a challenge to overcome. The other thing with hunting is that you, the hunter, are not usually the prey. This is not the case when it comes to self-defense. Let's not forget that you must know the hunting laws when you hunt, but you usually won't be investigated for a criminal act you've shot and killed your prey. So the legal mindset for hunters is also very different.

Pillar #5, and the one we are primarily concerned with here, is Civilian Self-Defense. First, what exactly is self-defense?

As stated earlier, Merriam-Webster defines self-defense as: *the act of defending yourself, your property, etc.; skills that make you capable of protecting yourself during an attack.* Personally, I actually disagree with the part about "your property, etc.". Our goals in self-defense are really simple; we need to go home, safe and alive, to our family at night.

Now, how does the mindset for self-defense differ from the mindset of all of the other pillars or backgrounds we have discussed? Good question. Here is how I see it. The self-defense mindset is "I must do what I have to do to get home to my family tonight." In a self-defense situation the violence is going to find us. We don't get to pick and choose when this will happen. We don't get to choose if there is one attacker or three, we don't get to choose if it happens in broad daylight or under the cover of darkness, we also don't get to choose where it happens, whether in familiar surroundings or in a strange place. We also don't usually have access to a radio to call for back up, intel on the ground, air support, camouflage, a good position for observation or enough training to get good hits fast. We are not likely to have our best and prettiest full size race gun within reach in our perfect race holster. We are more likely to be carrying our tiny sub-compact with the annoyingly long trigger pull stuffed into a slow, comfortable holster, which is in our waistband and covered by two or more layers of clothing at the time. It is also likely that we don't have spare ammo on this fateful day.

The other potentially more dangerous scenario is that we don't recognize the danger we are facing in time to do a whole lot about it.

We might have the training part on our side but, what about the confidence that we will get a good hit, or even remember our training? Do we know what a developing crime even looks like? Have we done our homework on the law and understand what might happen to us legally even if we did everything right? Do we understand the physical and emotional stressors that can arise in the wake of a self-defense shooting? How will we be treated by our friends and family? If you haven't thought of these things before, I beg of you, please, please, *please* be armed with this information and knowledge *before* it is too late. You are setting yourself up for a rude awakening if you *don't* consider these things when you are safe at home, relaxed and able to think about them critically and with the best information available. Once a self-defense scenario is actually happening, you don't have time to think about them.

Self-defense is where I am coming from in my approach to shooting. I prefer to think of my gun as a tool instead of a means to an end. When I train, I work hard at acquiring firearm skills, but I also train in other areas, such as learning how to recognize and understand how violence happens so that hopefully I can keep myself out of a violent encounter in the first place. If I never have to use my gun in self-defense, that is the best possible outcome!

To recap, does being the best soldier make you a good hunter, or vice versa? No, not necessarily, but *some* of the gun skills are definitely transferrable from one discipline to the next. You still need to be able to nail the fundamentals (Stance, grip, sight alignment, sight picture, hold control and breath control – if you've done any firearms work you will be familiar with these) with every shot. Only results matter, so I am not going to tell you *how* you *have* to shoot. If you can hit your target accurately and quickly, I don't mind which grip you decide to use. Again, people from all of these backgrounds can effectively teach someone how to shoot and hit a target; I am not disputing that. I would still encourage to you look inside yourself and know what *your* goals are and find a teacher with the right mindset and skills to help you get there. I don't care what type of background other instructors have; what I do care about is whether they can relate to what *your* goals are when it comes to shooting. If you want to become a tactical operator, SWAT member, or a huntress then I think that is great, but I won't be comfortable teaching you those skills. Yes, I know tactics, and could kill an animal if I had to, but those skill sets don't apply to me in my everyday life. I want to live my life day in and day out knowing that I have not altered the way I live in order to be able to defend my life and the lives of those I hold dear, if it should ever come to that. What are *YOUR* goals? If it's that you want to learn about firearms and their use for self-defense, then I'm your girl!

About the Author

Jenna Meek is a self-defense instructor specializing in the firearms discipline. She and her husband, Jeff run a firearms training school called Carry On Colorado located in the greater Denver area. The focus of Carry On Colorado is not just to teach the Gun Skills. They believe that taking a complete approach to self-defense is important. That's why they teach classes on recognizing and avoiding violence and gun skills in addition to teaching about the legal responsibilities of owning and using guns for self-protection and what happens in the legal aftermath of self-defense incident.

When Jenna is not teaching grownups, she is homeschooling her school aged son and battling the affections of her naughty yet ever so loving black Labrador retriever, Vader.

Visit CARRY ON COLORADO for Jenna's training website and keep up with the latest on her blog:

Jenna is Carrying On ... Again

https://jennacarryoncolorado.wordpress.com/

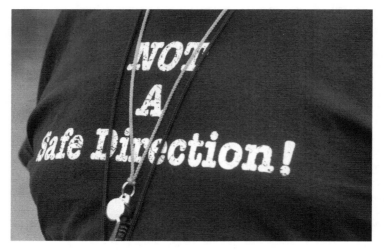

Photo by Tamara Keel of "View From The Porch".

Jenna also designed these T-Shirts as a fun way to remind people to be safe. The topic of gun safety is a very serious one, but there is no reason we can't also have fun while keeping people safe! Get your own "Not A Safe Direction" T-Shirt by visiting:

http://carryoncolorado.com/Apparel

If you enjoyed this book then please consider leaving a review on Amazon. Thanks!